July 31, 2007

Dear Bea,

It's good to know of someone like you who can remember the Detroit Tigers of the Hank Greenberg era. And I do appreciate all of the good things your two daughters do for me.

Best Wishes and God Bless!

Clayton Klein

A Well-Kept Secret

From the Glory Years of the Detroit Tigers

Clayton Klein

Wilderness Adventure Books
P.O. Box 856
Manchester, MI 48158
www.wildernessbooks.org

All photographs and drawings are from the author's personal collection.

Printed in the United States of America

To the Memory
of a
Loving Mother and Wife

Marjorie Nash Klein

Other Books by Clayton Klein

Cold Summer Wind	1983
One Incredible Journey	1985
A Passion For Wilderness	1986
Challenge the Wilderness	1988
Campfire Poems	1995
Cold Summer Wind II	2002

Acknowledgments

I wish to acknowledge these people and thank them for their support and assistance in helping to create this book.

Virginia Jonckheere Dayton for sharing her memories of Marjorie and Henry Greenberg.

Elnora Sharp Munsell for her memories of attending Tiger baseball games with Marjorie as they used tickets supplied by Hank Greenberg.

C. Robert Nash, Marjorie's brother, for information about their father, Maurice J. Nash.

Kenneth H. Nash, the younger brother, for his assistance in helping to solve the well-kept secret.

Robert 'Bob' Feller for sharing his memories of Hank Greenberg and Charlie Gehringer.

Jon Finlan for the information on coach Clem Spillane and his memories of baseball at Fowlerville High School.

Michael Grimm for supplying information about his uncle Charlie Gehringer and the Gehringer family.

Lynne McLean for keyboarding and helping to get the words right.

Jeanette Page for proof-reading and her helpful suggestions.

Denise Walters for keyboarding and keeping the author's house slick and clean.

Steve Horton of *The News & Views* with information about Fowlerville High School baseball, from the archives of *The Fowlerville Review*.

Darrell Klein for sharing memories from some of his younger years.

Debbie Klein for proof-reading and punctuation assistance.

Robert E. Smith for sharing his memories of Charlie Gehringer and the Gehringer family while growing up on a neighboring farm southeast of Fowlerville, Michigan.

George Winegar for his assistance with information and photos of his uncle Charlie Gehringer.

Contents

Introduction

This is the story of a well-kept secret, a secret lasting more than 64 years. Now it can be told.

The secret was kept by the author's wife of more than 61 years, Marjorie Nash Klein, along with her relatives and her friends. Neither was the secret revealed by her former friend, Detroit Tiger star and Baseball Hall of Famer, Hank Greenberg, in his autobiography, ***Hank Greenberg: The Story of My Life***, published by Triumph Books in 2001.

It was 21 months after her death when, with the encouragement of our son Darrell and daughter Debbie, I decided to begin to look through some of the dozens of old boxes their mother had stashed away around our house, mainly upstairs. I began investigating in December of 2004. Those boxes contained all sorts of items, old photographs, letters, and family history.

One day I happened upon a box holding a five-year diary along with the key. Other items found on following days included framed and autographed photos of Hank Greenberg, many Tigers game scorecards from the late 1930s and 1940s, two scrapbooks of newspaper clippings about Hank, and samples of "Home Run" letters that Marjorie had sent to him. I also discovered a stack of letters Hank had mailed to Marjorie during his years with the Detroit Tigers. Most of these finds I had not ever known existed. And there was more, much more.

My Marjorie had told me about her acquaintance with Henry B. "Hank" Greenberg before we were married, but she never did tell me how well acquainted they had been. She was the devoted mother of our two children and my wonderful wife for more than 61 years. So, imagine if you can, my consternation and concern as I read her diary and made these and many additional findings as I attempted to solve the mystery of Marjorie and Hank.

1

Those Home Run Letters

Marjorie Nash grew up on Guilford Avenue in eastern Detroit, Michigan. The family home was a brick house built by her father, Maurice J. Nash. In the 1920s and 1930s, the area was mainly rural even though the city of Grosse Pointe was only a mile away. Many of Detroit's early automobile executives lived in Grosse Pointe. Marjorie was the first born of five children in the Nash family with two sisters, Elizabeth and Evelyn, later followed by brothers Charles Robert and Kenneth Harold. The entire family, including mother Laura Eager Nash, was very musically inclined.

Marjorie was so talented that by the time she reached the age of three, she often sang solos for family guests accompanied on the piano by her mother. Later she and her siblings attended Sunday school and services at Grosse Pointe Memorial Church. There the three sisters frequently preformed, becoming known as "The Nash Trio." Marjorie first attended Hansteen School then went on to graduate from Edwin Denby High School on January 10, 1935. There she was voted the most talented girl in her class. She was also a fine pianist, making several appearances in the Kenneth W. Smith concerts at Detroit Conservancy of Music located on Woodward Avenue.

The Depression years in the early 1930s were financially difficult for the Nash family, along with people everywhere in all occupations. This was especially true in Detroit, known then as the automobile capital of the world. Grandpa Edwin S. Nash was a dairy farmer and breeder of registered Holstein cattle. He lived south of Howell, Michigan, where Maurice J. had grown up before finding work and moving to Detroit in 1917. Grandma Nash maintained a flock of laying hens and grew a field of strawberries. She had numerous customers in Howell for the eggs and grocery stores that purchased her sweet strawberries. While Marjorie was growing up, and during the remaining summers of her grandmother's life, she helped with the farm work including picking and sorting the berries.

Soon after graduating from Denby High, Marjorie enrolled in Wayne State College. Money was scarce but from babysitting for family friends, she had saved enough to pay the $10.00 tuition fee for her first semester. Her favorite subject was art. She was soon doing pencil drawings from photographs as well as nude models who posed for the class. Many of the art classes were held at The

Detroit Institute of Arts, which was just a short walk across Woodward Avenue from the college. She was fortunate to witness Diego Rivero painting the huge murals of Mexico on the Institute walls. By the time she entered Wayne State, Marjorie had developed into a fun loving, well mannered and charming young woman. She was full of personality with those pretty blue eyes sparkling under her glistening red hair.

Like most of the people living in the Detroit area and many living across Michigan and southwestern Ontario, Canada during those years, the Nashes were all Detroit Tigers fans. Everyone had heard of Ty Cobb, who had recently hung up his spikes. They all knew about the iron man of baseball, Lou Gehrig, and home run king Babe Ruth of the Yankees. They also all knew about the young Tigers second baseman Charlie Gehringer, who had grown up on a farm southeast of Fowlerville, Michigan, a town next to Howell.

Henry Benjamin "Hank" Greenberg, born January 1, 1911, was a native New Yorker. He was the son of Rumanian born Jewish immigrants who owned a successful cloth-shrinking plant. Hank told Marjorie that he grew up at 663 Crotona Park North in New York City, New York and graduated from James Monroe High School in the Bronx, then attended New York University for one semester before beginning his professional baseball career.

His six-foot, four-inch tall, 215-pound athletic success stemmed from size and hard work. His high-school coach explained, "Hank was so big for his age and so awkward that he became self conscious. The fear of being made to look foolish drove him to practice constantly and, as a result, to overcome his handicaps." Hank tried out for the New York Giants but manager John McGraw, although constantly on the lookout for a Jewish star to attract New York's large Jewish population, decided that Hank was too clumsy and uncoordinated to help the Giants even though Greenberg's powerful hitting had impressed him. Hank later turned down a lucrative offer from the Yankees, realizing there would be little chance of making the team with Lou Gehrig on first for the Bronx Bombers. He also rejected an offer from the Washington Senators.

Greenberg signed up with the Tigers in January of 1930. After minor league stops in Hartford, Raleigh, Evansville, and Beaumont, he was called up to the Tigers in 1933. Still awkward in the field playing first base but quick on his feet, he showed line drive power. In his rookie year, he batted .301, drove in 87 runs and homered 12 times. This gave him a lot of publicity in newspapers and on the radio.

The broadcaster for radio station WWJ in Detroit was Ty Tyson. Hank Greenberg soon became the talk of the town, attracting the attention of thousands of Tigers fans everywhere. One young woman in particular, who picked strawberries in the summertime, and her friends were especially impressed with the unusual abilities of this new young Tiger first baseman.

When the 1934 baseball season opened, the Tigers soon surged into first place in the American League. Marjorie was so interested in the games that she soon talked Grandma Nash into a break each summer afternoon while the Tiger games were in progress. She and the picking crew could then go to the house and listen to the game on the porch radio while they sorted the berries. Elnora Sharp was one of the berry pickers who became Marjorie's lifelong friend. "Someday I'm going to find a way to meet Hank Greenberg," Marjorie confided in Elnora. "Right now I don't know how or when but he's great and I must find a way." Her desire increased during the summer as the Tigers finished the season seven games ahead of the second-place Yankees. Hank led the team with 139 runs batted in and a batting average of .339 while smashing out 26 home runs. The Tigers lost the World Series to the St. Louis Cardinals in a seven-game series in which Hank batted .331 while driving in seven runs.

H.G. Salsinger of the *Detroit News* wrote, "The development of Greenberg is one of the most amazing features of an amazing baseball season. He was a good hitter last year, and a long one, but today he is one of the most powerful sluggers who has come along in years. The unusual feature of his development is that Greenberg's fielding has improved with his hitting."

In later years Hank wrote in his book, ***Hank Greenberg: The Story of My Life***, "A truly exciting moment in my Major League career took place on September 10, 1934, Rosh Hashanah, the Jewish New Year. The team was fighting for first place, and I was probably the only batter in the lineup who was not in a slump. However, in the Jewish religion, it is traditional that one observes the holiday solemnly, with prayer. One should not engage in work or play. And I wasn't sure what to do. It became a national issue. There was a big question in the press about whether I would play first base for the Tigers that day. On the front page of that morning's *Detroit Free Press* was a headline in Yiddish, and then over it in the English translation, 'Happy New Year, Hank.' To this day I am very proud of that."

Hank continued, "The newspapers had gone to the top Rabbi in Detroit and asked him if it would be sociably right for me to play on that day. He came up with the theory that since it was the start of a new year and it was supposed to be a happy day and Jews had played games on that day, he felt that it would be perfectly all right for me to play baseball. That momentous decision made it possible for me to stay in the lineup on Rosh Hashanah and, lo and behold, I hit two home runs, the second in the ninth inning, and we beat Boston 2-1."

Bud Shaver wrote, "Greenberg probably never before hit a ball as hard as he hit that second pitch. Hank met the pitch perfectly. The ball sailed on a line, cleared the wall beyond the scoreboard and Henry trotted around the bases as the crowd swarmed onto the field. At the plate, Hank was met by a milling throng and it was with difficulty that he made his way to the club house."

Ten days after Rosh Hashanah comes another Jewish holiday. Yom Kippur was another important decision for Greenberg. It is the most sacred holiday of the year for Jews. Yom Kippur is their day of atonement. On September 18, the *New York Times* wrote that the Tigers had the American League pennant all but "signed, sealed and delivered," and that Hank, batting .338 with 25 home runs, "was the most important cog" on the team. This time he chose not to play.

"I was a hero around town," Hank wrote in his book. "Particularly among Jewish people, and I was very proud of it. On Yom Kippur, my friends, a family named Allen, took me to the synagogue. We walked in about 10:30 in the morning and the place was jammed. The Rabbi was praying. Right in the middle of everything, everything stopped. The Rabbi looked up; he didn't know what was going on. And suddenly everybody was applauding. I was embarrassed, I didn't know what to do. It was a tremendous ovation for a kid who was only 23 years old and in a synagogue no less!"

Hank continues, "People remember that I didn't play on Yom Kippur. They remember it every year, but in fact the situation arose only once, in 1934. It's a strange thing. When I was playing I used to resent being singled out as a Jewish ballplayer, period. I'm not sure why or when I changed, because I'm still not a particularly religious person. Lately though, I find myself wanting to be remembered not only as a great ballplayer, but even more as a great Jewish ballplayer. I realize now, more than I used to, how important a part I played in the lives of a generation of Jewish kids who grew up in the thirties."

Edgar A.Guest, the nationally syndicated newspaper poet, was known by his Detroit neighbors as "Eddie Guest." Marjorie had saved a copy of one of his poems published in the *Detroit Free Press* in 1934. Marjorie stashed a copy of this poem in her autograph scrapbook.

SPEAKING OF GREENBERG *by Edgar A. Guest*

The Irish didn't like it when they heard of Greenberg's fame
For they thought a good first baseman should possess an Irish name;
And the Murphys and Mulrooneys said they never dreamed they'd see
A Jewish boy from Bronxville out where Casey used to be.
In the early days of April not a Dugan tipped his hat
Or prayed to see a "double" when Hank Greenberg came to bat.

In July the Irish wondered where he'd ever learned to play.
"He makes me think of Casey!" Old Man Murphy dared to say;
And with fifty-seven doubles and a score of homers made
The respect they had for Greenberg was being openly displayed.
But on the Jewish New Year when Hank Greenberg came to bat
And made two home runs off Pitcher Rhodes—they cheered like mad
for that.

Came Yom Kippur—holy fast day world wide over to the Jew—
And Hank Greenberg to his teaching and the old tradition true.
Spent the day among his people and he didn't come to play.
Said Murphy to Mulrooney, "We shall lose the game today!
We shall miss him on the infield and shall miss him at the bat,
But he's true to his religion—and I honor him for that!"

Marjorie received a belated graduation gift of a five-year diary in which she recorded the most memorable events of her young life, beginning on March 12, 1935. The earliest entries of interest are as follows:

> *April 27-We got word at four this morning that Grandpa Nash had died.* [Grandpa Nash was Edwin S. Nash of Howell.]

> *June 15-The Tigers won a double-header from the Athletics, 10-1 and 11-3, Hurray!*

> *June 28-Hank Greenberg hit three home runs in a double-header with St. Louis.*

Edgar A. Guest

Early in 1935, young Marjorie came up with an idea that she hoped would attract the attention of Hank Greenberg. Her plan was to send him a little note every time he hit a home run. She would draw a silhouette of Hank swinging his bat and connecting with the ball, adding his number 5 on the back of his shirt as in the picture on page 18. She would write the number of each home run in the season on the ball leaving his bat. Placing the card in a little handmade envelope measuring 2½ x 4 inches, she would address it simply to Navin Field, Detroit. She enacted her plan at the start of the 1935 season. She mailed them each with a two-cent stamp the morning following the game. These "Home Run Letters" continued for the next six years.

By the All Star Game, the Tigers were leading the American League. Hank led the League in home runs before the mid-season classic and proceeded to set a record with 110 runs batted in.

Marjorie kept busy in her spare time preparing and mailing those little home run letters.

Her diary recorded the Tigers' triumphs and failures.

> *July 8-The American League won the All Star Game.*

Tigers fans could not understand why Hank was not selected to play in the game. The year before he had produced 26 home runs with 139 runs batted in. Now at All Star Game time he had driven in 110 runs and still wasn't selected. This also had to be a puzzlement for Henry Greenberg.

Hank once said to *Free Press* columnist Joe Falls, "When I first came to Detroit, I stayed at the Wolverine Hotel for $8.00 per week. They gave me a room and bed with the bathroom down the hall. It wasn't so bad because we took most of our showers at the ballpark...The big deal was at the Detroit Leland. They served a complete dinner and had a full orchestra. I had to decide whether it was worth a dollar and a quarter per day. Plus you had to leave a 25-cent tip. I thought about it all the time and finally said, "Aw, let's give it a try." The truth is, they had a good-looking waitress there and I was hoping I could impress her with a 25-cent tip."

July 13-The new hired man at Grandma Nash's, Steve Lipka, is a nut, if I do say so.

Aug. 19-Uncle Norman and Aunt Francis visited us in the evening. [Norman Nash was a brother of Maurice J. Nash.]

Sept. 13-I drew a picture of Hank Greenberg.

Sept. 19-I mailed Hank's picture to him. I sure hope he'll autograph it for me.

About this time, Marjorie began doing pencil drawings of sports figures and movie stars. In the envelope with the picture, she would include a note asking the person she sketched to please autograph the drawing and return it to her.

Sept. 23-First day of school at Wayne State. Hank sent my picture back autographed. He also sent me a card. He's a swell guy!

Oct. 1-I'm sending a picture to Ty Tyson for an autograph.

Ty Tyson made the first broadcast of a Detroit Tigers game in 1927 from Navin Field. He continued calling the plays on radio station WWJ through 1942 when he turned the mike over to the former Tiger star Harry Heilmann.

Oct. 2-Chicago Cubs won first game of the World Series from Tigers. Lon Warneke did a swell job of pitching.

The Tigers had won another American League pennant finishing three games ahead of the Yankees. As 47,391 people filled the stands, Schoolboy Rowe lost the first game for the Tigers.

It was the largest crowd ever to watch a ball game at Navin Field. Hank had finished the 1935 season with a .328 batting average, coming to bat 619 times. He batted in 170 runs with 46 doubles, 16 triples and 36 home runs.

Oct. 3-Tigers won the second game.

Hank Greenberg was injured!

The Tigers started the game, scoring four runs in the first inning. Greenberg homered with Charlie Gehringer on first base scoring the winning runs. In the seventh inning, Hank tried to score on a hit from second base. Gabby Hartnett had the plate blocked as Hank slid, breaking Hank's wrist, as Hartnett fell in the collision.

Oct. 4-Tigers won game in 11 innings. Eldon Auker, Chief Hogsett and Schoolboy Rowe were the Tiger pitchers.

Oct. 5-Tigers won the game. General Crowder was winning pitcher.

Oct. 6-Tigers lost, 3-1. Schoolboy Rowe pitched again.

Lynwood "Schoolboy" Rowe was born in Waco, Texas in 1910 and began pitching for the Tigers in 1933. He picked up his nickname as a teenaged sandlotter. Rowe became one of the American League's top right-handers in 1934 when this broad-shouldered Arkansan compiled a 24-8 mark to lead the Tigers to their first pennant. Schoolboy was a hard worker with a fastball that did tricks. He even talked to the ball while pitching. He once said, "During my 16-game consecutive winning streak, I would eat a lot of vitals, climb on that mound, wrap my fingers around the ball and say to it, 'Edna honey, let's go.'" Edna Rowe was also the name of Schoolboy's wife.

Rowe retired from baseball in 1949 with a career record of 158-101, and died in El Dorado, Arkansas at age 50. Charlie Gehringer once said of Schoolboy, "He could hit a baseball as far as Babe Ruth—and I always thought 'Schoolie' had a fastball as good as Grove's."

Oct. 7-Tigers won the World Series Championship. I sent a picture to Charles Gehringer to autograph.

Oct. 24-Got my drawing of Charlie Gehringer back, autographed.

Nov. 13-Frank Navin died this morning.

Nov. 14-I started a Hank Greenberg scrapbook.

The scrapbook, measuring 10 x 15 inches with 103 pages, is on the author's desk this morning. It is full of articles and photos of Hank, clipped from the three Detroit daily newspapers, the *Free Press*, the *Times* and the *News*. There are also mementos from the *Saturday Evening Post* and New York's *World Telegram*.

The back cover of the scrapbook holds dozens of additional loose photos and articles about Hank. Some of the writers of these stories include sports writers W.W. Edgar, Tod Rochwell,

The first Home Run envelopes of each year, 1937-1940, which Hank Greenberg saved and eventually returned to Marjorie.

Doc Holst, Les Macdonell, Charles P. Ward, Sam Greene, Bob Murphy, H.G. Salsinger, Henry McLemore, Malcome W. Bingay, Daniel M. Daniel, Bob Considine, and Stanley Frank.

Dec. 7-I worked on a Christmas card for Hank about seven hours.

Dec. 13-Went shopping after classes. Saw 'Goose' Goslin at Hudson's. Shook hands with him, ha ha.

Jovial 'Goose' Goslin was the Tiger star center fielder from April of 1934 through 1937. Most likely 'Goose' was also Christmas shopping at J.L. Hudson's the afternoon Marjorie met him there. Goslin broke in with the Washington Senators in 1921 and by the time the Tigers acquired him in 1934, he had developed a reputation as a powerful clutch hitter with an accurate and strong throwing arm. On June 6, 1934, he saw his 30-game consecutive hitting streak end as the Tigers won the game with only one hit, a single by Charlie Gehringer. 'Goose' Goslin batted in 100 or more runs in each of his first three years with the Tigers and had a lifetime batting average of .316 during his 17 seasons in the American League. He was voted into the National Baseball Hall of Fame in 1968.

In an article in the *Detroit Free Press* in 1935, Hank Greenberg tells W.W. Edgar one reason his Tigers lost the 1934 autumn classic to the Cardinals was fear. Fear that the team would look bad. He went on to say, "There are some pitchers who put a scare into me. I get scared even before I ever step to the plate—afraid that I won't be equal to the task." He continued, "There was the opening game of the World Series against the Cardinals. Do you remember that nightmare? We took the field knowing that we had to face Dizzy Dean, and it was the first World Series in Detroit in 25 years. All this helped frighten us and we played like a high-school team. Even such a capable and unemotional player as Charlie Gehringer booted the ball all over the field until we finally settled down. Then it was too late." Hank could have also mentioned a few other American League pitchers of whom he was afraid, such as Rapid Robert Feller of the Indians and Lefty Gomez of the Yankees, who each struck him out on numerous occasions!

In August of 1935, the author was one of ten young men chosen from Fowlerville High School to see a Tigers game. Baseball coach John Baker, along with local businessmen Walter S. Tomion and Thomas E. Woods, drove us to Navin Field. There were no school busses in those days. Before game time we were introduced to Charlie Gehringer, the Tigers' second baseman. Charlie was a 1923 graduate of Fowlerville High School.

2 The National Pastime

Marjorie's diary from 1936 offers more details of the young artist's life:

Jan. 1-Hank's Birthday!

Jan. 4-Got a Christmas card from Hank Greenberg.

Jan. 13-Went to school. We drew from a live model in art class. I was the first one finished.

Jan. 20-Felt lazy in art class. King George of England is dead.

Jan. 27-Drew from a Chinese model in Art class. Tommy's cute.

Feb. 2-Sunday School and church in morning. I drew Clara DeMitchell a picture of Charlie Gehringer. [Clara DeMitchell was one of Marjorie's close friends. They attended both school and church together through their teenage years.]

Feb. 29-Mother and Daddy went to Howell. Those two bully sisters of mine think they're smart. Sometimes I just hate them.

Mar. 16-Hank hasn't signed up yet. Wish he would hurry and do it.

Hank was having trouble negotiating with the new Tigers owner, Walter O. Briggs, who was also the C.E.O. of Briggs Manufacturing Co. Hank requested a salary of $35,000. The club offered $25,000. In his book, ***Hank Greenberg: The Story of My Life***, Hank wrote, "Mr. Briggs got very annoyed with my demands, so for the first and only time in my baseball career, I became an official holdout. When spring training started, I was among the missing."

Mar. 19-Went alone and saw 'Rose Marie,' the most marvelous picture I've ever seen.

April 23-Auker pitched a shutout, 10-0. Good for him. Hank's back!

Eldon Auker pitched for the Tigers from 1933 to 1942. He was a submarine pitcher and had developed his underhanded style of pitching because of a shoulder injury he had suffered while playing football at Kansas State University, where he had studied pre-med. When he graduated in 1932, good jobs were hard to find. "As I had played halfback in football," he said, "I was offered a contract by the Chicago Bears. I wanted to play baseball in the summer and football in the fall, but Mr. Navin said no. I liked football better but I chose baseball because the season was already underway and Mr. Navin was paying me $400 a month."

Auker's underhand sinker made him a winning pitcher with a 15-7 record in 1934 and an 18-7 mark in 1935. He was the losing pitcher of game seven of the 1934 World Series for the Tigers. He lost the game to Dizzy Dean of the St. Louis Cardinals after winning game four of the series. He was a good-hitting pitcher, compiling a .308 average in 1936. In fact, on August 14, 1937 he hit two home runs while beating the St. Louis Browns 16-1. He was traded to the Red Sox late in 1938, where he pitched the first two years of Ted Williams' career. Then traded to St. Louis Browns, Auker retired from baseball in 1943. He settled down in Vero Beach, Florida and died on August 4, 2006.

Eldon Auker

April 24-Tommy Bridges pitched Tigers to a victory, 9-3.

Tommy Bridges was the son of a country doctor. He graduated from the University of Tennessee and was expected to follow his father's example. He chose baseball instead, and the only doctoring he did was intended to induce sharp, breaking curves. Bridges' frail appearance was deceptive. Though he had a blazing fastball, his curve was the wonder of the American League for over a decade, according to the Baseball Library.

Charlie Gehringer once said, "Tommy Bridges was as good as Hal Newhauser. I've seen him throw that curve ball at a guy's head, and the batter would fall flat on his rear end thinking it was going to hit him, and then the ball would go over the plate for a strike."

Tommy was a big hero in the 1935 series. In the sixth game of the Series, the Cubs looked like they might beat the Tigers. The score was tied in the ninth inning when Stan Hack led off with a triple against Bridges. Tommy reached back and retired the next three men without Hack being able to score. The Tigers scored in the bottom of the ninth when Cochrane reached second base and with two outs, Goose Goslin singled him home to win the Series for the Tigers. After the game and the title, Cochrane was lavish in his praise of Bridges. "A hundred and fifty pounds of courage. If there ever is a payoff on courage this little 150-pound pitcher is the greatest World Series hero." The city of Detroit celebrated into the wee hours of the next day, according to Ralph Burger.

During the 1930s, Bridges was named to the American League All-Star staff six times, and gained a victory in 1939. With 194 career regular season victories, four in the World Series, and one in an All-Star game, Bridges had 199 career wins. After his playing days, Tommy became a combination coach and scout for the Cincinnati Reds in 1951, and scouted for the Tigers from 1958 to 1960. His last job in baseball was as a scout for the New York Mets from 1963 to 1968. When he wasn't in baseball, he spent time as a tire salesman in Detroit. He died on April 19, 1968 in Nashville, Tennessee.

April 29-Hank Greenberg's wrist is broken again! He'll be out for more than a month. That darn Jake Powell ought to be shot for colliding with Hank and breaking his wrist!

May 5-The papers say that Hank's wrist is broken in two places. Oh! Me!

June 18-Elizabeth's graduation exercises in evening. Grandma Nash and other folks came from Howell.

June 19-Began picking berries at Grandma Nash's.

June 20-Went to a barn dance with Sorgs and Bob Buell.

June 27-Tigers won the ball game, 8-4. I sure got a sunburn today.

Aug. 4-Went to a Tiger game and had grand seats. Hank worked out even though his injured wrist was taped up. He's swell!

Marjorie had only one Home Run Letter to send in 1936. On April 29, Hank was leading the league in RBIs and hitting .350 when Jake Powell of the Washington Senators crashed into him, breaking the wrist again. Hank was sidelined for the rest of the season even though he tried to keep in condition. More than a year later, Daniel M. Daniel, writing in the New York *World Telegram*, observed that the crowd in Navin Field "booed Powell every time he came to bat. A Detroit paper had run a story questioning whether possibly Powell, having put Greenberg out for the season last year, could have been accidental."

Sept. 11-Mickey Cochrane sent my picture back, autographed.

"Since 1909 Frank Navin never had been able to get another Detroit Tiger winning combination clicking," wrote Malcolm W. Bingay, editor of the *Detroit Free Press* in his book ***Detroit Is My Own Home Town***. By 1933, with the bank crash rocking him to the foundations, Navin was in despair. He had lost a carefully built-up fortune, the team was not getting anywhere, and the fans were howling for new ownership. All washed up and ready to quit, he went to his partner, Walter O. Briggs.

"Walter," said Navin on that afternoon in '33, "Let's quit. I'm sick of it all. Jim Murfin was in to see me yesterday. He represents a syndicate headed by Ty Cobb. They want to pay us two million for the club. That'll fix me for life."

"I'm not selling," said Briggs promptly, "and you're not selling. What we need is a new manager."

"Who can we get?"

"Well, there's a fellow on the Philadelphia club I'm sold on. He'll win pennants for us. He's a fighter. Why the other day I saw him start to climb right into the stands to get at Patsy O'Toole for yelling at him. That's what I like—a fighter."

"You mean Mickey Cochrane?"

"Yeah, that's who I mean. Get him."

"How can we get him? Connie Mack will want a hundred thousand dollars for him and we haven't got a hundred thousand cents on hand."

"That's all right. I'll pay for him. I want him. I'll lend the club what is needed to get him. You just get him and we'll win a pennant."

They made the now-historic deal. A testimonial dinner was given after the World Series to honor Navin and Briggs. A few days later, Navin dropped dead of heart failure. The pennant fight and the banquet were too much for him. After his death, under Briggs, baseball ceased to be just a game in Detroit, it became a business.

Sept. 21-I've landed a job. I'm going to work for the F.C. Smith store up on the corner of Warren [F.C. Smith was a chain of grocery stores in the area.]

Sept. 22-Uncle Norton was here for a couple of hours. Tigers won a double-header from St. Louis, 12-0 and 14-0. Oh! Boy!

Sept. 30-Carl Hubbel pitched grand ball and Giants took first game from the Yankees, 6-1.

Oct. 6-The New York Yankees won the World Series. I was kinda disappointed 'cause I'd rather have seen the Giants win.

Nov. 3-Elnora was here in the evening. While we were at the bowling alley, Harold Wright walked in. We roasted marshmallows when we got home. [Harold Wright was a friend and neighbor of Grandma Nash.]

Nov. 26-Grandpa and Grandma Eager were here for Thanksgiving dinner. [Lyman and Gertrude Eager were the parents of Laura Eager Nash.]

Dec. 17-I mailed my package and card to Hank. Here's hoping he likes it as well as I enjoyed making it for him.

Dec. 27-We listened to Nelson Eddy in the evening and he was grand!

Elnora Sharp [Munsell], Marjorie's lifelong friend, in 1942

Now for a few Diary entries from 1937:

Jan. 4-Harold Wright is the nicest fellow I've known yet.

Jan. 5-I got the swellest letter from Eddie Guest along with the picture autographed. He's grand!

Jan. 12-Went to movie at the Colony and saw 'Rose Marie' again. It's the fourth time for me.

Feb. 6-Grandma Nash has finally decided to go to Florida, and it's Lakeland! "Hello Hank!"

Feb. 11-Elizabeth is on her way to Florida with Grandma Nash, and Rosie. (So I didn't get to go!) [Rosie was Marjorie's nickname for her Uncle Norton Nash.]

Feb. 19-Pop's Birthday. (He's 40) so we had a swell supper.

Elizabeth Nash's photo of Hank Greenberg at spring training

Mar. 15-I'm so excited! Elizabeth sent pictures of Tigers and my 'Hankus' posed with her, for me. Oh! Dear me!

Mar. 29-I spent most of the afternoon drawing a picture of Hank.

Apr. 15-We went and heard and saw Nelson Eddy at the Masonic Temple. He was simply marvelous.

Apr. 20-Opening Ball Game. Gerry Walker was the game's hero.

Apr. 23-Hank hit his first homer.

Apr. 28-Tigers won the ball game, 11-5.

May 2-Frances Sharp brought four girls from Howell to go to the ball game with Elnora, Elizabeth, and I. We had good seats just beyond first base and my binoculars came in handy 'cause Hank was so close. After the game we went out onto the playing field and took photos of each other. I readily admit it's the most fun I ever had at a ball game.

May 3-Hank hit a home run with the bases loaded. Boy! I'm so proud of him!

May 13-Oh! Boy, we have a new Nash [automobile].

May 21-My Hank is coming right along. He hit his 5th homer today.

May 22-Hank hit No. 6 today.

May 24-I got my picture back from Dizzy Dean and a grand letter from a Cardinal official.

Jerome "Dizzy" Dean was the Ace of the Gashouse Gang, the nickname of the St. Louis Cardinals during the 1934 World Series with the Detroit Tigers. In the regular season, Dean had racked up 30 wins with only seven losses. His brother Paul Dean, nicknamed "Daffy," was also on the roster.

Dizzy liked to brag about his prowess and make public predictions. Dizzy predicted, "Paul an' Me are gonna win 45 games." On September 21, Diz pitched no-hit ball for eight innings against the Brooklyn Dodgers, finishing with a three-hit shutout in the first game of a double-header for his 27th win of the season. Paul then threw a no-hitter in the nightcap, to win his 18th to match the 45 that Diz had predicted. "Gee, Paul," Diz was heard to say in the locker room afterward, "If I'd a known you was gonna throw a no-hitter, I'd a thrown one too!" He was also fond of saying, "If you can do it, it ain't braggin'." Dizzy finished with 30 wins, the last National League pitcher to do so, and Paul finished with 19, for a total of 49. After the season, Dizzy Dean won with the National League's Most Valuable Player Award.

Diz had one more prediction: "Me an' Paul are gonna win this here World Series." Diz won Game 1 and Paul won Game 3. However, during Game 4, Diz played as a pinch runner, and was hit in the head by an errant throw from Tigers shortstop Billy Rogell. Dizzy told the press, "The doctors x-rayed my head and found nothing." He pitched the next day but lost Game 5. Paul won Game 6 and Diz pitched a shutout to win Game 7.

Here are a few other quotes by Dizzy Dean:

"The good Lord was good to me. He gave me a strong body, a good right arm and a weak mind."

"Sure I eat what I advertise. Sure I eat Wheaties for breakfast. A good bowl of Wheaties with bourbon can't be beat."

"I ain't what I used to be, but who the hell is."

"Son, what kind a pitch would you like to miss?"

"It puzzles me how they know what corners are good for filling stations. Just how did they know gas and oil was under there?"

"I won 28 games in 1935 and I couldn't believe my eyes when the Cards sent me a contract with a cut in salary. Mr. Rickey said I deserved a cut because I didn't win 30 games."

Dizzy Dean was elected into the Baseball Hall of Fame in 1953. He died at age 64 in Reno, Nevada. The Dizzy Dean Museum is located in Jackson, Mississippi.

May 25-*Mickey Cochrane was hit in the head and has a fractured skull.*

The Great Depression had brought catcher and manager Mickey Cochrane to the Tigers in 1934. Connie Mack was disassembling his dynasty in Philadelphia for financial reasons and sold

Cochrane to the Walter O. Briggs team. Cochrane led the Tigers to the World Series in 1934 and 1935. His playing career ended suddenly on May 25, 1937 when a ball thrown by Yankee pitcher Bump Hadley struck him in the head. The injury nearly killed him and he never played baseball again. He was only 34 years old. Cochrane returned to the dugout but had lost his competitive spirit. He managed for the remainder of 1937 and was replaced midway through 1938. In 1999, he ranked number 65 on the *Sporting News* list of 100 Greatest Ball Players.

Cochrane was a close friend of fellow baseball legend Ty Cobb and Cobb was a good friend to Mickey, helping him out financially near the end of his life. Mickey Cochrane and Ray Schalk were the only baseball players to attend Ty Cobb's funeral. Cochrane was elected into the Baseball Hall of Fame in 1947 and died in Lake Forest, Illinois at the age of 59.

Career Highlights of Mickey Cochrane:

- Won American League Most Valuable Player in 1928 and 1934
- Played in five World Series
- Hit over .300 for a season nine times
- Scored the game-winning run in game six of the 1935 World Series to lift the Detroit Tigers to victory over the Chicago Cubs

May 27-Hank hit his 7th home run and was forced from the game with a strained leg muscle.

June 3-Our First Concert went over big, and so did the Nash Trio.

June 4-Hank hit his 13th homer.

June 8-Hank hit no. 15!

July 7-The American League All Stars won the game. Hank sat on the bench while Gehrig played 1st base.

Aug. 4-I got my picture back from Jimmy Stewart, autographed. Now to try some more stars.

Marjorie's Autograph Scrapbook measures 12 by 16 inches and contains 38 pages with two of her pencil drawings on nearly every page. The title page reads "Autographed Pictures by Marjorie Nash" followed by "Sports-Radio-Movies."

The first page contains autographed pictures of Mickey Cochrane and Hank Greenberg. Page two contains more drawings of Hank. Page three has autographed pictures of Charlie Gehringer and Lou Gehrig, who wrote above his signature, "To Marjorie—With Kindest Regards." In a P.S. below, he wrote, "Your work is most flattering."

And so it goes. The pictured stars personally autographed most of her pencil drawings. These athletes also signed their portraits: Rudy York, Joe DiMaggio, Eldon Auker, Buck Newsom, Marvin Owen, "Goose" Goslin, Gerry Walker, Dizzy Dean, "Schoolboy" Rowe, Charles Grimm, Gabby Hartnett, Johnny Allen, Lefty Gomez, Larry Aurie and Earl "Dutch" Clark.

There are signed pictures of Edgar A. Guest, Lowell Thomas, Ty Tyson, Fred MacMurray, Allan Jones, Nelson Eddy, Jeanette MacDonald, Robert Taylor, Barbara Stanwyck, Clark Gable, Bette Davis, Jimmy Stewart, Claudette Colbert, Randolf Scott, and Tyrone Power. Also included are drawings of Amos and Andy, Spencer Tracy, Loretta Young, Errol Flynn, and President Franklin D. Roosevelt.

The Autograph Scrapbook also contains autographed black and white photos of Fred MacMurray, Gary Cooper, Clark Gable, Barbara Stanwyck, Jeanette MacDonald, and Gerry Walker, plus several of Hank. He signed the photo he gave her on September 28, 1938 with, "To My Friend Marjorie With sincere Best Wishes, 'Hank' Greenberg."

Aug. 13-Hank hit his 26th today and it is Friday the 13th!

Aug. 17-Barbara and Joanne are here and they are the best little kids! [Barbara and Joanne are daughters of Norman and Francis Nash, Norman was a brother of Maurice J. Nash.]

Sept. 6-Labor Day. Mother, Dad and I went to Navin Field to see the double-header. Hankie hit a home run. The Goose did a lot of clowning around before game time.

Sept. 7-I drew pictures of Hank all afternoon.

Sept. 8-Hankie hit two home runs in the 2nd game, 34 and 35. Ain't he just grand?

Oct. 3-A pitching duel between Jake Wade and Johnny Allen.

Oct. 7-I got my picture back from Jeanette McDonald, autographed!

Greenberg saved all of Marjorie's home-run cards and shared these homemade envelopes with a reporter.

On August 4, 1937, the Tigers were stuck in a five-game losing steak and suffering from a shortage of healthy catchers. Manager Mickey Cochrane decided to try Rudy York, who had been their rookie without a position. Little did anyone know that this would be the start of one of the most remarkable stretches for any player in the history of baseball. In his first game as a catcher, he responded to the opportunity by going two for five with a three-run home run and four runs batted in.

York started every game except one as catcher for the rest of the month. On August 30, his 16th homer helped the Tigers beat the New York Yankees 5-4. On the final day of the month, this 24-year-old catcher hit one far over the left field fence into Cherry Street in the first inning to equal Babe Ruth's record of 17 home runs in one month. Then in the sixth inning, York swung again, walloping the ball even harder over the left center field scoreboard, collecting his second homer of the afternoon. That blow broke Ruth's record of 17 home runs established in 1927. Along with those 18 homers, Rudy York batted .360 with 49 runs batted in for the month of August. This record stood for more than 60 years until Sammy Sosa, who hit 20 homers in June of 1998, broke it.

In ***Hank Greenberg: The Story of My Life***, Greenberg writes, "Having the rookie slugger Rudy York follow me in the batting order was helpful. With him behind me, I got more good balls to hit, pitchers were not so ready to walk one, knowing that the next batter they'd have to face is likely to hit the ball out of the park," This arrangement worked well for both Rudy and Hank for a couple of years.

Then in January of 1940, Hank received a notice from Tigers' General Manager, Jack Zeller, wanting to have Hank come to Detroit to discuss plans for the coming season. Zeller's plan concerned both Rudy York and Hank. Rudy was no longer catching as well as management expected and he could not cut it in the outfield. They felt his natural position was at first base and they wanted to keep Rudy in the lineup because of his ability of hitting the long ball. Consequently, in order to strengthen the lineup, Zeller had decided to move Hank to the outfield. This surprised Hank, as he had never played any position other than first base in the majors. Hank went home to think it over, and then came back with a few suggestions. Soon they drew up and signed a contract. If Hank could be in the lineup in left field on Opening Day, he would receive a bonus of $10,000 in addition to the salary he received in 1939.

On September 24, Bill Slocum wrote in the New York *American,* "If Detroit does win the pennant...it will be more for the common sense of Greenberg than even the power he packs in his ringing bat. For Hank did something that few ballplayers would do. Something that to my knowledge, no other Major League player has ever done before in quite the same way. He gave up a position in which he was an outstanding star and which he preferred to play for the good of the Detroit team."

Rudy York and Hank became the best of friends. These two were the sparkplugs that led the Tigers to the American League championship in 1940. Rudy played first base for the Tigers through 1945. Then he was traded to the Boston Red Sox and Hank moved back to first base. York died of lung cancer in 1970 in Rome, Georgia at the age of 56.

The Tigers failed to make it to the World Series in 1937 even though Hank had one of his best years. He came to bat 573 times, playing in 148 games. He drove in 150 runs with a batting average of .340, connecting for 41 home runs. He was voted the American League's Most Valuable Player.

These were the years when baseball was still a game and certainly the National Pastime. Baseball and the National Hockey League were then the only organized sports. Several more years would pass before the National Football League and the National Basketball Association would come into existence.

Imagine, if you can, what life was like for sports fans during the first half of the twentieth century. There was no television. Listening to the radio had only become popular after 1925 and soon most families had a radio in their homes. In rural areas, their radios were battery powered and needed a long outside antenna. Baseball games were only played in the daytime. Lighted ball parks became popular after 1936.

There were the college sports of football, basketball, and baseball. And yes, the Olympic Games came along every four years. There were the occasional heavyweight prizefights featuring World Champions like Jack Dempsey, Max Baer, Joe Louis, and Max Schmelling. For a few, there was golf. But baseball in the American and National Leagues was the primary sports activity of interest to most people in the U.S.A.

Charles Grimm

Gerry Walker

Larry Aurie

Lefty Gomez

M·NASH
To-"An admiring Fan, and
a real sport", (Marjorie)
"Buck" Newsom,
Detroit Tigers.

"Buck" Newsom

Charlie Gehringer

M. NASH
To Marjorie—
With Kindest
Regards—
Lou Gehrig
P. S. Your work is most flattering—

Lou Gehrig

Mickey Cochrane

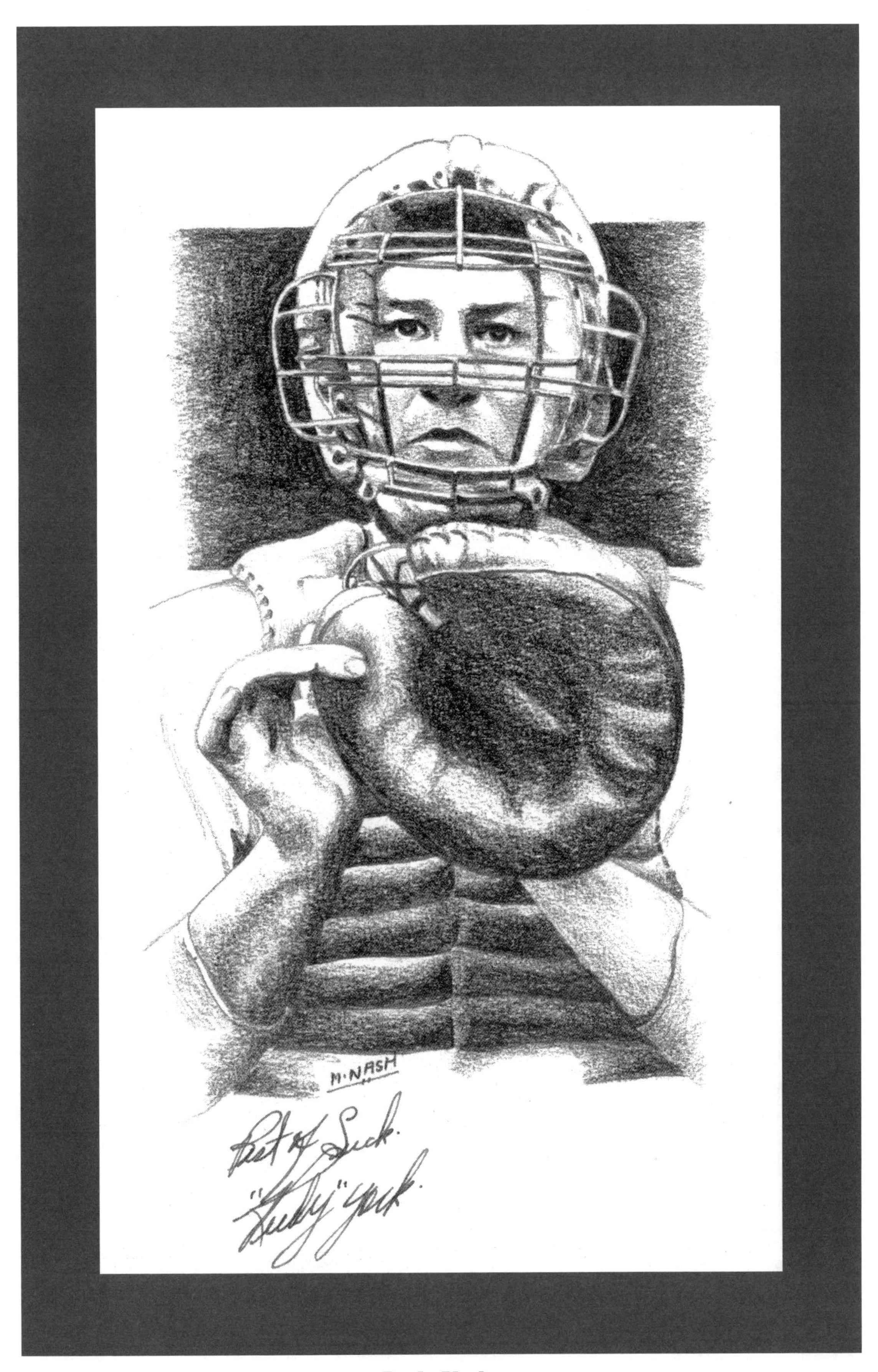

Rudy York

"Schoolboy" Rowe

"Goose" Goslin

Friday May 21st/37

St. Louis National Baseball Club

Cardinals

Dr. Harrison J. Weaver

Offices
3623 Dodier St.

Saint Louis
Missouri

My dear Miss Marjorie — I feel obliged to tell you how much "Dizzy" and in fact all my 'Gang' enjoyed your drawing of him. I, personally, saw him autograph it and, while he doesn't usually indulge in such "Spencerian Flourishes" he really did himself proud on your drawing.

I took it upon myself to wrap it for mailing and trust it was returned to you in good condition.

Thanking you for your interest in him —

Sincerely
Harrison J Weaver.

P.S. Yes, we would like to play your Tigers in the October Classic. Can't you make it possible?

"Dizzy" Dean

Johnny Allen

Hank Greenberg

Joe DiMaggio

James Stewart

Lowell Thomas

Barbara Stanwyck

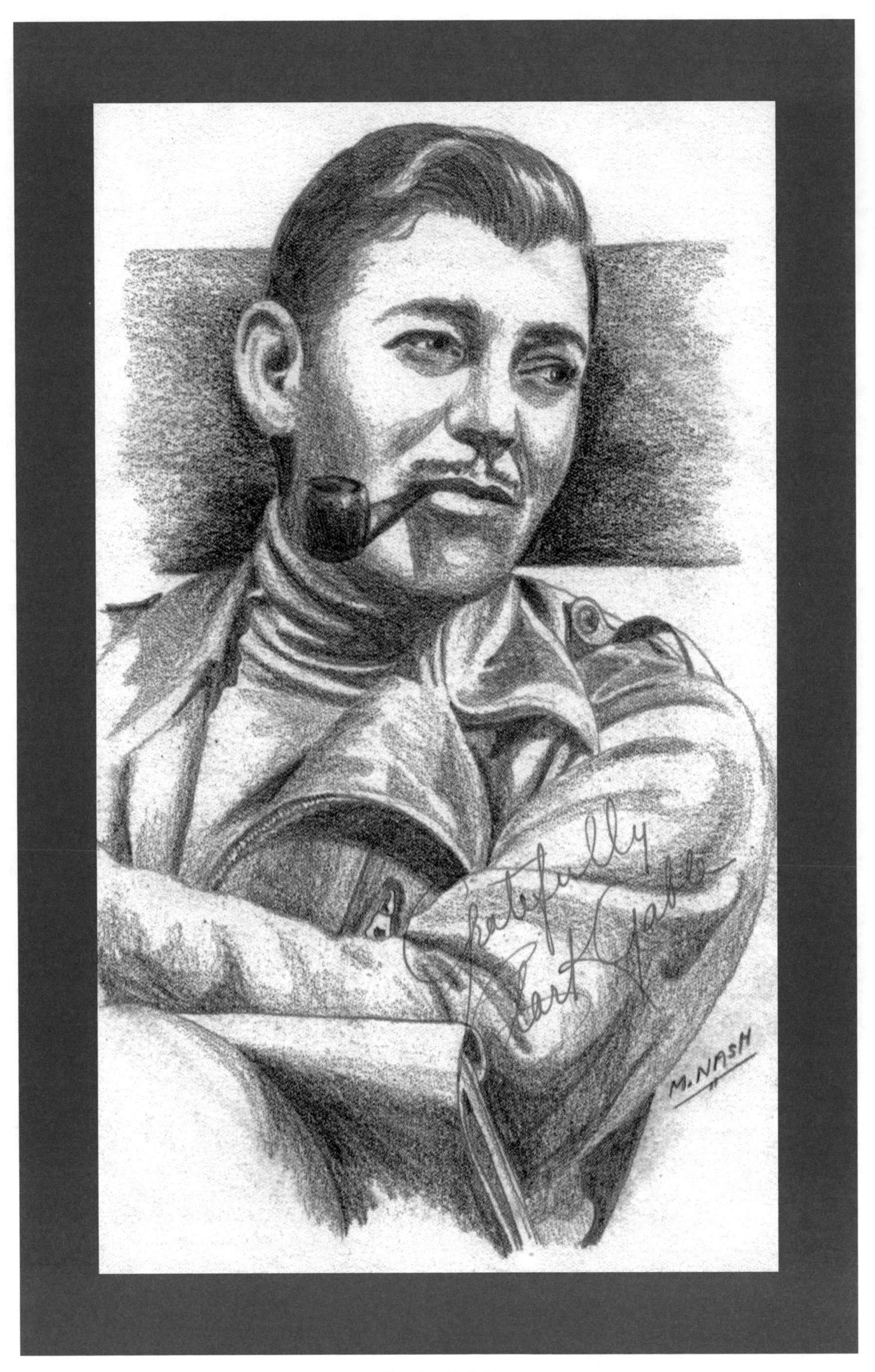

Clark Gable

Bette Davis

Allan Jones

Claudette Colbert

Fred MacMurray

Robert Taylor

Nelson Eddy

Jeanette MacDonald

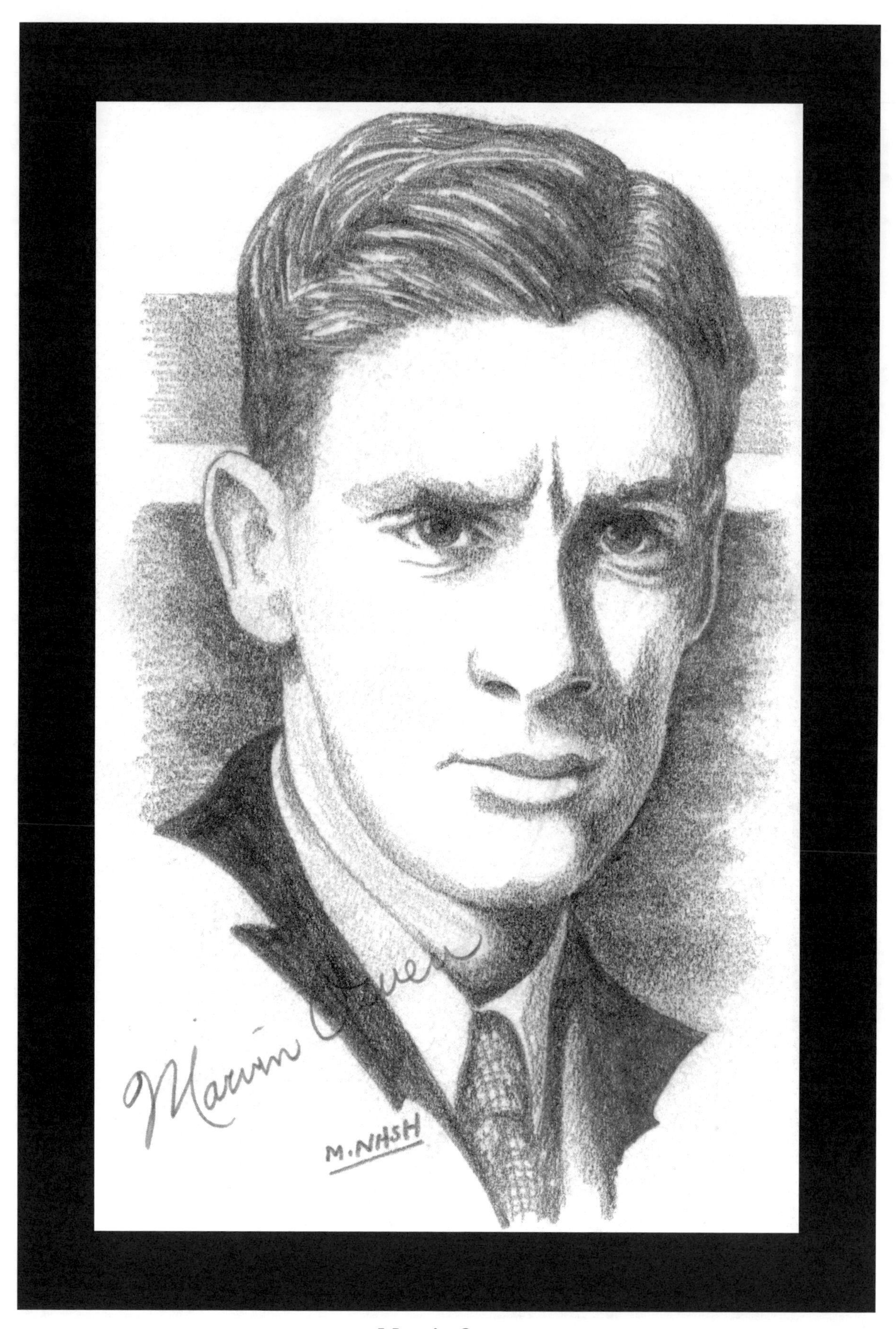

Marvin Owen

Dreams Do Come True

Feb. 4, 1938-I spent most all day working on more comic cards for Hank's home runs.

Feb. 11-Spent all day drawing pictures of Hank! Ahem.

Apr. 19-The Tigers lost the opener but Hankie hit his 1st homer.

Apr. 23-Elnora and Frances Sharp came down in the afternoon to stay all night.

Apr. 24-It rained just before game time but we saw Bob Feller beat the Tigers.

May 15-Another rainy day. How is Hank going to hit any home runs?

June 14-Hank hit #14.

July 23-Worked all day at store. Got a pay raise to .40 cents an hour.

On May 25, the Tigers use the long ball to defeat the Yankees, 7-3. Rudy York and Hank each hit back-to-back homers twice in the game.

July 26-Hankie hit two of 'em today.

July 27-Two more home runs chalked up by Hank.

Hank was doing well. After hitting two homers in his last two times at bat the day before, he homered his first two times at bat on July 27 to tie the Major League record of four in a row.

July 28-Hank hit two more homers.

On August 6, with the Tigers in fifth place in the American League and 17 games out of first, Walter O. Briggs fired manager Mickey Cochrane, replacing him with Del Baker. Under the new manager, Hank's home run total for the season reached 41 on August 19.

Now there was much talk that Hank might be able to break or tie Babe Ruth's 1927 record of 60 home runs. Henry was certainly off to a good start, as Ruth did not hit his 41st until August 27.

On August 31, Greenberg hit No. 46 in Yankee Stadium. There were 32 games left in the season and he still needed 14 homers to tie the record.

Everyone across the country, including Marjorie, her family, and her friends were hoping, wondering, and asking, "Will he make it?" Speculation continued with each remaining game.

> *Aug. 7-Hank Greenberg must have enjoyed my stick-men drawings so well that he permitted some of them to be printed in the Sunday edition of the* Detroit News. *Ten of them were reproduced along with the envelopes with one or two little balls. I guess most everyone I know saw them. I'd give most anything to meet Hank, and perhaps some day I will!*
>
> *Aug. 31-Dossie Beasley bought us all ice cream.* [Dossie Beasley married Marjorie's sister Evelyn in 1940.]
>
> *Sept. 7-A* Detroit Times *reporter called to see if he could interview me about my scrapbook. Here's hoping he comes.*
>
> *Sept. 11- Hank hit No. 48 and No. 49!*
>
> *Sept. 13-A* Detroit Times *photographer and reporter were here and took pictures of me.*
>
> *Sept. 14-Mr. Vanson brought me two box seat tickets for tomorrow's Tiger/Yankee game.*
>
> *Sept. 15-Elnora came down to go to the game with me. We had a marvelous time. I took pictures of Hank, Ty Tyson, Billy Rogell and Eldon Auker.*

Another of Marjorie's favorite players on the Tiger team was Billy Rogell. William George "Billy" Rogell was a major league shortstop primarily of the Detroit Tigers. The combination of Rogell at shortstop and Charlie Gehringer at second base was a key factor in the Tigers' success in the 1930s. The Tigers went to two World Series in 1934 and 1935, winning their first title in franchise history. Rogell led all AL shortstops in fielding percentage for three years, between 1935 and 1937, and in assists for two, in 1934 and 1935. He was the Tigers' Opening Day shortstop for the 1932 season, a position he would hold for the next eight years. A sure-handed fielder, he and Hall of Fame double-play partner Charlie Gehringer would give the Tigers one of the best keystone-combinations in baseball history. Marv Owen, who would man the left side of the Detroit infield with Rogell for five years, said of Rogell's fielding prowess, "He's the only player I ever knew who could catch a bad hop...I don't know how he did it."

After losing in seven games to the Cardinals, the Tigers returned to the series the following season. Again led by their stellar infield, the Tigers won the pennant by three games over the Yankees and earned a trip to face the Chicago Cubs for the world championship. Rogell finished with another solid year at the bat, hitting .275 with 88 runs scored while drawing 80 walks. Although he

Every Time That Henry Greenberg Hits a Home Run

the Postman Delivers Another Sketch

HENRY GREENBERG has a pen and ink sketch for every home run he hit this season. The artist is Miss Marjorie Nash, 4550 Gilford street, Detroit. She sends him one each time he hits a home run. The sketch comes in an envelope that has a silhouette of Greenberg completing his swing in the lower left hand corner, a ball with the number of the home run and addressed to "Briggs Stadium—Det." His name has never appeared on an envelope but all the sketches have been delivered to him. Ten of them are reproduced had shown speed in the minors, Rogell rarely had a chance to move on the bases with Detroit. "They didn't want me to steal," he would say after retiring. "I had Gehringer and Cochrane and Greenberg hitting behind me." Rogell led American League shortstops in fielding percentage in 1935, '36, and '37. He also led the league once in both putouts and assists, and twice paired with Gehringer to lead the league in double plays. The two played over 1000 games together, making them one of the longest tenured double-play combinations in the history of the game.

Rogell spent the bulk of his "retirement" as a member of the Detroit City Council. After a brief stint in the minors as a player and coach, he returned to Detroit and began his civil service career in 1942. Rogell, after leaving the council, spent the rest of his retirement in Detroit. At age 94 he threw out the first pitch at the final game at Tiger Stadium on September 27, 1999, nearly 70 years after he had debuted for the Tigers in the same park. Billy Rogell died of pneumonia at the age of 98 in the Detroit suburb of Sterling Heights on August 9, 2003.

Sept. 16-I sure would like to get to know Hank Greenberg.

Sept. 18-Elnora and Frances came down and we went to the ball game again. Tigers won 9-1.

Sept. 21-Hank hit Number 54!

Sept. 22-Hank hit Number 55 and 56!

Sept. 25-Clara DeMitchell stopped to see my scrapbook.

Sept. 26-Clara talked me into writing a note to Hank to ask if I could see him for a few minutes to give him my scrapbook. Please Hank! Don't turn me down!

Sept. 27-I got a letter from Hank, asking me to come down to the Leland Hotel to see him! Hank hit No. 57 and 58 today. "He's one swell fellow."

Sept. 28-The Big Day!

The author found the following typed on nine pages and neatly folded to fit inside of Marjorie's diary box below the five-year diary:

DEAREST DIARY,

I MET HANK GREENBERG! I shall write on your very choicest pages an account of my most exciting day, Wednesday, September 28, 1938, for on that day my fondest dream was realized.

The Sunday before, Clara DeMitchell suggested that I write Hank Greenberg a note, addressing it to his hotel, and ask him if I could meet him for just a few moments to give him an addition to the scrapbook of drawings I had sent him in 1936. Hank's answer came by return mail, and that is when I lost my healthy young appetite. (Ain't it oreful?) It finally seemed that a five-year-old dream was to be realized.

Early Wednesday morning I boarded the bus, headed for the Leland Hotel, armed with a scrapbook of drawings representing two years of transferring Hank from newspaper photographs to pencil drawings.

I arrived at 9:45 and immediately called up to his room but the operator told me that Hank was receiving no calls until after 10:00 o'clock. I sat down over next to the wall so I could see everyone who came and went, and in about 10 minutes a tall, good-looking young man entered the lobby and walked over to a man who was sitting down and apparently waiting for him. It was HANK! My heart took a flip-flop and I felt positive that I could never muster enough courage to approach him. I stalled too long, for they left the lobby and went down the stairs to the Coffee Room. I followed close behind and then took up sentry outside the lunchroom door until Hank should again appear.

He did, in about 45 minutes, and he headed straight for the stairway. That is where I entered the picture. I went up to him, held out a card with its tiny silhouette of him on it, and almost in a whisper, I asked for his autograph. He took one look at the card and Oh, dear diary, you should have seen the expression on his face. It was worth a million dollars! He turned on that captivating smile of his and exclaimed, "So you are Marjorie!" My bad case of stage fright deserted me. In the face of such a warm and friendly welcome, how could I remain frightened and ill at ease? We shook hands at the foot of the stairs, and Hank talked all the way up, remarking about my other scrapbook and saying that he had been wanting to see me for the last two years (He's as bad as I am). One of the first things he asked me was, "What are you doing this afternoon?" When I answered, "Nothing after two o'clock," he told me that he would leave a ticket for the ball game for me at gate 14, that is, if I wanted to go, but dearest diary, you wouldn't condemn me just because I said "yes," would you?

We walked over to the desk in the lobby while Hank picked up his mail, and then, after glancing through it, he invited me up to his rooms where we would be uninterrupted, so he said. When I hesitated (I was thinking of Emily Post), he laughed and said

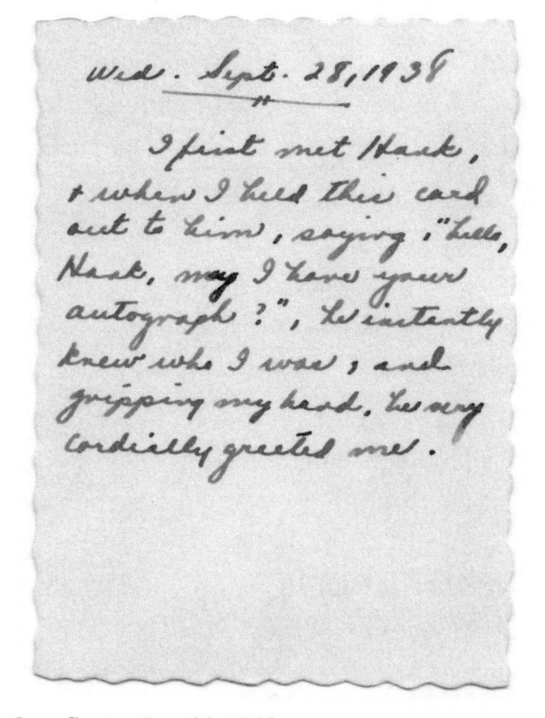

Wed. Sept. 28, 1938

I first met Hank, + when I held this card out to him, saying, "Hello, Hank, may I have your autograph?", he instantly knew who I was, and gripping my hand, he very cordially greeted me.

The front and back of the card Hank Greenberg recognized on September 28, 1938.

that it was quite proper, so we headed for the elevators. While walking toward them (and we leisurely strolled) he kept repeating that he didn't see why I wasted my talent drawing pictures of him, while if I told him once I told him five times that it was not wasted time and talent. I said that I enjoyed drawing more than anything else in the world, and he made a very nice subject to draw.

His rooms were on the 12th floor, at the back of the hotel, and as he unlocked the door and shoved it open he said, "To the left, and please overlook those scattered newspapers until I get them picked up." I sat down in a cozy upholstered chair and watched him pick up newspapers, while he chatted and for all the world looked like a small boy getting a great kick out of life. After he had seated himself on the davenport, I handed him my drawings.

It was fun watching him while he looked them over, exclaiming about each one and picking out and remarking about those he especially liked. He is a very intelligent young man, and he certainly follows Hank Greenberg via the newspapers. He had seen them all in the papers, and he said that many of them were a big improvement over the originals. It made me feel that all my effort had not been in vain. He remarked that he was going to take them home (to New York) and have them all framed. When I laughed at him, he said, "All right, when you come to New York come to my home and I'll show them to you." After looking through them twice, he asked me what I would do if he were traded to the Yanks, and when I said I didn't know he said, "I suppose you read that article in the *Free Press* the other day, but there is not a bit of truth to it." Coming from him, who could ask for a more direct answer, and one that was the most certain to be the truth.

We got to talking about fan mail, and I asked him what he did with his, for he certainly must get a lot. He said that he threw it all away, everything except mine, and to prove it he took from his desk a little pile of letters, all the home run letters I sent him. (Oh boy, do I rate.) He wanted to know if I had seen them in the paper, and when I said "yes," he asked me how I thought they reproduced. I remarked that they were not as distinct as they could have been, while he added, "No, and the color wasn't there either."

He explained how they happened to be printed. It seems I sent him an extra funny home run letter one day, and while he sat in the locker room laughing at it a reporter happened by. Hank showed him a few of them and he immediately wanted to take some pictures of them to publish in the *News*. Hank seemed very proud of them, but no prouder than I was when I saw them.

He asked me if I would like a picture of him, and when I said "yes," he got up, took a folder of photographs from a desk drawer, and handed them to me to look at. While I looked through them and picked out two that I especially liked, he got a huge envelope from somewhere and sat down again on the davenport to show them to me. They must have been about 12" by 18", and had been given to him by a friend of his who is a sports photographer for the *News*. They were all action shots taken at the games, with Hank of course, as the center of interest in each picture. As he handed them to me one by one, he explained each picture and laughed with me at the funny things in some of them.

Suddenly the telephone rang! Hank politely excused himself and got up to answer it. While he was talking, I glanced thru the latest edition of the *Sporting News* that sported his picture on the cover. The hotel operator was on the phone to tell Hank that someone wished to see him, but he said to tell whomever it was that he couldn't be reached. He no sooner put the receiver down than it rang again. This time a friend of his from up higher in the hotel wanted to see him before 12:00 (it was then 11:30). I couldn't keep from smiling at Hank when he said that he would try to make it, and when he saw me smile he grinned in return.

After his friend hung up, Hank picked up the two pictures I had selected, added another from another collection that he said was his favorite, and sat down to autograph them for me. Then he spied the picture he had taken of the home run letters I had sent him, and asked me if I would like it. I thought perhaps he might want to keep it himself because he had told me earlier that the photographer had taken it at his special request, but he insisted that I take it, adding that he had the newspaper pictures of them and also the originals.

Then he began rummaging around for a ball to autograph. I had always wanted an official American League baseball, and it seemed that I was about to get one. Finally he found a brand new one, still in the box, and he had rather a difficult time trying to clamp it between his knees to write on it. While busy writing on first the ball and than the pictures, we talked about his home runs. In a very amused voice he asked me if I was sorry I had followed his home runs this year, and when I asked him why, he replied that I'll bet I didn't know he would hit quite so many. I laughed and said that I still had two envelopes left. "That is all you are going to need," he laughed, and when I said that I hoped he would hit 60, he only said that time would tell, and that he would be in there trying every day.

I said, "Well, if you don't make it this year you are just as liable to do it next year or the year after." Golly, then he did laugh, and cracked "What is that old saying about one bird in the hand is worth two in the bush? I would have 58 to get all over again."

I had an excellent opportunity to inspect his attractive bachelor's quarters while he once again tackled his autographing. Venetian blinds hung at the windows, and a wine colored rug covered the floor. A small round table stood in the center of the room with a huge bowl of assorted fruit on it which, Hank had explained when we entered the room, the hotel manager had sent up just after he had hit 57 and 58 the day before. Two closed doors opened off of the sitting room, and I gathered that one led to the bathroom while the other opened into the bedroom. Everything was strictly masculine, even to the electric clock on his desk.

Those pictures were finally autographed (he must love to write or he wouldn't have spent so much time at it) and as Hank got up from the desk he found an envelope in the top drawer to put the pictures in. Then he handed them to me. I thanked him for everything he had done for me and he laughed as I added that we acted like a pair of old friends. As he stood there, hands in his pockets, looking down at me, he added that he wished there was something else he could do for me. He said that I had done so much for him and had gone to so much expense following his home runs. I emphatically told him that I wanted nothing in return, and that just meeting him and receiving such a warm reception was plenty of reward for me. He smiled at that, and again invited me down sometime after he got back from New York, to talk baseball and what have we. As an afterthought he added, "And bring your girlfriend." He could tell, it seemed, that I was not in the habit of visiting men in their hotel rooms alone.

At about 10 minutes to 12, I glanced at my watch and, seeing how late it was getting, I stood up and said that I had better get going or I'd be late for classes. Hank looked at his watch also, but instead of moving toward the door, he went over to a corner table and picked up a huge scrapbook sent to him by a young admirer, and he asked me if I wanted it. I replied that I would like a good picture of Lou Gehrig and Babe Ruth and that I might find them in there, so Hank came over to where I was standing and began leafing through it to see if he could find them. He remarked that he couldn't imagine why the kid had sent him the scrapbook, for some of the pictures in it were actually ancient. We stood so close together there in the center of the room that when he hesitated at a page to show me some picture, his sleeve brushed my cheek as I tried to see what he was trying to show me. He is certainly tall and well built, with broad shoulders, powerful arms, and long tapering fingers denoting very expressive hands. He is just twice as good-looking in street clothes as he is in his baseball uniform, and golly, I had always thought, in drawing him, that he certainly couldn't be any handsomer, but I soon discovered differently.

We finally got started for the door, and as he stepped aside for me to exit first, I remarked that his rooms were indeed very attractive, while he answered that they were nice and cool, and for him I suppose that is what mattered the most.

As we walked down the hall toward the elevators, I glanced up at him and asked him in what section of the stadium the seat would be.

One of the autographed photographs Hank gave Marjorie at their first meeting.

He laughed down at me and replied, “Oh, I think I’ll put you in the bleachers.” I made such a face at that remark that he said, “Now you really don’t think that I would put you way out there, do you?” How was I to know where he would put me, but I answered that I didn’t think he would do that.

When we finally reached the elevators, he pressed the down button for me and waited with me until it should arrive. It did, all too suddenly, and as the door opened, he put his arm across my shoulder, gave me an affectionate pat on the shoulder and a gentle shove, and reminded me again not to forget to be at gate 14 for the ticket he would leave. My last glimpse of him as the door closed was his arm upraised to wave goodbye, and that nice smile of his lighting up his face. (His smile, to me, is his nicest feature, although his eastern accent is darling and his incessant chatter is very entertaining. He has that “gift of gab.”)

I got out to the ballpark at 2:30, and I walked directly up to gate 14 and asked the gateman for the ticket left for Miss Marjorie Nash. He glanced into the ticket box, shook his head, and answered that there was none. My disappointment must have registered on my face, for he smiled and very kindly asked me who was to have left it. I said that Hank Greenberg was to have left it, and at that, he turned around to a man who stood behind him and spoke to him. He asked me to come in where he was, and then he told me that it was too late to get ahold of Hank, but there were plenty of unoccupied seats, so I could go right in and take my pick.

I stopped to buy a scorecard, and then I went in search of Mr. Henry Greenberg. I didn't want any seat; I wanted the one that Hank had promised me, and I was determined to talk to him and find out, if possible, why he had failed to leave it.

As I walked along the runway behind the Tiger dugout Hank saw me, waved, and hollered, "Did you get the ticket all right?" I stepped down into the box seats to talk to him but a man suddenly popped up from one of the seats and would have halted me if Hank hadn't said that he wanted to talk to me. When I stood before him I laughed up at him, tipped my hat back, and said, "Well, that's the first time I ever crashed any gate on my looks." At that, a surprised look passed over his face and he again asked if I had gotten the ticket with no difficulty. Then I told him that there was none. It suddenly dawned on him that he had forgotten to leave it, and he called to the batboy and asked him to run down into the clubhouse and get it from his pocket.

After the batboy had disappeared, Hank apologized for his lapse of memory, and he said that he hoped I hadn't had to buy a ticket. I assured him that I hadn't, and then sat down to wait while he chatted with a reporter. When the ticket arrived, Hank handed it to me with "You are right behind the dugout where you can see me." (That was just where I wanted to be, but I didn't tell him that.) I thanked him as prettily as I knew how, and he tipped his cap and said good-bye as I turned and left the box.

I sat beside Tommy Bridges' mother, a dear little gray-haired lady with a very southern accent, while his wife was seated on the other side of her. Some more of the Tigers' wives sat in front of us but I didn't recognize them. Eldon Auker stood talking quite a few minutes with Mrs. Bridges and when Tommy was presented with a new cream-colored Buick convertible coupe, his mother was the proudest lady in the ballpark.

The Tigers won the game 12-0 but Hank hit no home run for me, and he did say before game time that he would try his darndest. He glanced my way several times as he stepped down into the dugout, and once he nodded as I waved my scorecard at him. I had a grand time and now I can truthfully say that I really know Hank, 'cause just as he said, Dear Diary, we are now old friends.

Marjorie's Christmas Gifts

Oct. 2-*I stayed home to listen to the ball games, and then Hank didn't hit any more, so he finishes the season with 58—not bad.*

It was this game, October 2, 1938, when Hank faced 19-year-old fireballer Bob Feller pitching for the Cleveland Indians. Bob established a Major League record by striking out 18 Detroit Tigers in a single nine-inning game. The only Tiger hit in the game was Hank's double off the left field wall.

Oct. 3-Got a letter from Elnora. She was almost as thrilled over me meeting Hank as I was.

Oct. 13-Drew two pictures of Hank. My, if I keep this up I'll have a huge scrapbook to give him next year.

Oct. 21-Worked all day on a layout for the design of the envelope for Hank's Christmas card.

Marjorie was thinking ahead with the design. On November 17 and the following three days she worked on Hank's Christmas card. She happily attended classes at Wayne State and continued working at the store until Christmas.

Oct. 30-Went to church with Elnora. We tramped the woods all day and we really had a heart to heart talk. Rode back to Detroit with Harold Wright. Darn it, I like him!

Now that she had met Hank, it's apparent Marjorie had seriously begun to let her mind wander and turn to the topic of other young men in her life.

Nov. 4-Went to a dance in Howell. I danced several times with Ed Holmes.

Nov. 25-Went to a box social at Chester Clark's. I had a marvelous time with Ed Holmes.

He bought my box and it cost him $1.50.

Dec. 2-I had the grandest time at the dance. We danced together most of the time.

Dec. 3-Ed came at 8:00 and we drove to Lansing, to the Coral Gables dance hall. Golly, I like to dance with him.

Dec. 16-We went to the dance at Oldfellows Hall. Ed danced with Ruth Latson a lot. Probably to make me jealous. Anyway he took me home after ice cream at Eager's Restaurant.

Dec. 23-Golly, I'm so happy I could cry. Hank Greenberg sent me a darling little lapel watch and three exquisite bottles of French perfume for Christmas. I don't see how some people can be so nice and live.

The final year of the five-year diary was 1939. Here are a few more of the select entries:

Jan. 10-Went with Sharps (Elnora and Frances) to the JFB meeting. As usual all the fellows gathered around Elnora and me, and of course Ed was one of them. Everyone admired my watch that Hank gave me. [JFB was The Junior Farm Bureau, an organization of young people who were growing up on farms across Michigan. Many in this group later became farmers.]

Jan. 14-The sleighing party at Latsons was some fun. Ed asked me to sit with him. We did more fooling around. Once when the sleigh stopped, Ed, Charles Latson and Ld Marshall dumped me off into a snow bank.

Jan. 16-The JFB meeting was lots of fun. I sure like that group. Ed seems to like me real well.

Jan. 23-Twelve of us went over to Bancroft to help organize the new Shiawassee County JFB.

Chester Clark drove and Elnora, Frances and I went with him. I think Chester likes me very much. He seems interested in everything I do.

Jan. 27-I had a very nice time at the dance. Ed was there. I danced quite a bit with Ralph Peckens and Charles Latson.

Mar. 1-Randolf Scott autographed my drawing. "In deep appreciation." Wasn't that nice of him?

Mar. 22-Elnora wrote to tell me that Ed Holmes is married. Well, I wish him luck...he'll need it.

April 13-Had a nice time at the JFB dance. Being married doesn't seem to have changed Ed Holmes one bit. His wife is awfully sweet.

April 18-Opening Ball Game and it rained during most of the game. It still didn't keep away 49,000 fans. Tigers won, 6-1.

April 20-Hank hit No. 1 in 14th inning to win the game from Chicago, 8-7. Yippie!

April 23-Schoolboy Rowe shut out Cleveland, 8-0, for his first victory.

April 26-Hank hit No. 2 and No. 3 today. What do you think of that?

May 2-Wowie! The Yanks sure skunked the Tigers, 22-2.

May 3-Hank hit No. 4. Golly, I sure hope he likes those stickmen cartoons I send him.

June 4-Norton took me to the ball game and we had swell seats. I was so furious at those 40 some thousand fans who booed Hank...I could have sworn.

June 9-Elizabeth and I went downtown shopping and stopped at the Leland to say hello to Hank. He seemed very pleased to see me and he insisted that we have breakfast with him. Golly, he was swell! He gave us tickets to the game in the afternoon and we were out there at 1:45 to watch batting practice. I was so tired when I got home, but very happy!

June 12-Hank hit two again yesterday so I have to get those Home Run letters off.

June 15-Hank sent me a card in a Centennial envelope marked "1st day of issue" from Cooperstown, NY. Wasn't that nice of him? Golly. He's always doing something nice for me.

June 27-Tigers lost the night game in Cleveland, 5-0. Bob Feller was terribly fast.

June 30-Buck Newsom pitched the Tigers to a 3-1 victory over Chicago.

July 1-I got my drawing back from Buck Newsom, autographed. He called me last night to tell me how much he liked it, and then ask me if I'd draw him one to keep. That telephone call was the most surprising thing that ever happened to me.

One of Marjorie's favorite Tiger pitchers was Louis "Buck" Newsom. Most people called him Bobo, because that is what he called everybody else. He was one of those great pitching characters such as Dizzy Dean, Lefty Gomez, and Satchel Paige.

This good ol' country boy was born in Hartsville, South Carolina in 1907 and as a rookie with the St. Louis Browns, won 20 games including a no-hitter that he lost with two out in the tenth. Bobo had the honor to pitch the opening game for the Browns in 1936 in Washington in front of President Franklin Roosevelt. In the third inning, his third baseman whipped a ball across the diamond and Bobo forgot to duck. The ball caught him on the side of the face. Clutching his head, he staggered in agony. His manager offered to take him out. "Naw," Newsom said "Ol FDR came to see Bobo and he's gonna see him all the way." He won the game 1-0. After the game, they found his jaw was broken in two places. It had to be wired shut.

"Buck" was traded to the Tigers in 1940 and won 20 games to lead the team to their first pennant since 1935. Management rewarded him with a $35,000 contract, topping Bob Feller who had been the highest paid pitcher in the game. Bobo hustled into the Tigers front office to sign the contract with Walter O. Briggs, brushing past Briggs' son Walter "Spike" Briggs, Jr. "Out of the way Little Bo," he said. "Big Bobo wants to talk to me."

Newsom also pitched game seven of the 1940 World Series, only two days after his father died while visiting and watching his son win game five. Then "Buck" fell on bad times, losing 20 games in 1941 as Tiger General Manager Jack Zeller cut his pay to $12,500 and in the winter sold him to the Dodgers. Upon learning this, Bobo wired Dodger manager Leo Durocher, "Wish to congratulate you on buying pennant insurance."

He died in Orlando, Florida at age 55 and was buried in his home town of Hartsville, which has a street named in his honor. Some of the facts about Newsom were provided by John B. Holway.

July 25-Mother forwarded a letter to me from Hank, and did it ever please me. He said he was very disappointed when no home run letters arrived and how pleased he was to get them. Then he asked me to come down to the game again as his guest. Golly he's nice!

Sept. 4-Hank hit "2" today.

Sept. 7-Finally got three pictures drawn for Buck Newsom and sent them to him. Bet by now he's given up all hope of ever receiving them.

Sept. 10-Hank called to tell me he was leaving two tickets for the double-header for me at the gate. Then he asked me to come down to the game again as his guest. Oh! But he sounded so nice and friendly.

Sept. 14-The folks drove Evelyn and me to the ballpark. We had the swellest seats, right among the Tiger wives.

Sept. 16-Hank hit No. 28.

Oct. 2-Hank sent back the pictures of himself and Rudy York, autographed.

The Tigers finished the season in fifth place, even though Hank had 33 home runs with a batting average of .312 while coming to bat 500 times and batting in 112 runs.

Nov. 17-I'm a little early this year getting my card ready to send Hank.

Dec. 2-Worked on some bookmarkers for Hank.

Dec. 22-Got a Christmas card from Hank. Mailed mine to him on the same day he sent the one to me.

Thus, we come to the final entries in the five-year diary, except for three additional pages for 1940 inserted inside the book's back cover. Consequently, there are no other diary entries for the year.

Jan. 4-Oh! Golly-just got home and opened my gift from Hank. It's a darling little 'Pick-me-up' Victor radio. Gee it's cute. Gus and Virginia Jonckheere were both here

Virginia Jonckheere [Dayton] in 1940

when I opened it. They thought it was swell also. Golly, why is Hank so good to me? Here I was so glad to get his Christmas card, and I never dreamed of such a gift as a little radio.

April 29-Mr. Vanson again gave me box seats to the ballgame. I took Virginia Jonckheere with me. We got out to the park at 2:00 and sat for a while watching the Tigers on the field. Finally they all came into the dugout and Hank passed right in front of us. He soon reappeared again, this time to pose with a small boy for a photographer. Virginia and I left our seats and stood just in back of Hank in the aisle, watching him and talking with the head usher. When Hank turned after having his picture snapped, I waved my hand and called "Hello, Hank." He acted so very surprised but glad to see me. He smilingly said "Hello there, Marjorie," took off his cap, tucked his glove under his arm and extended his big hand to clasp mine. He stumbled and almost fell into the dugout and we laughed merrily at his apparent clumsiness. We exchanged a few remarks. I asked him if No. 1 had safely arrived and then I introduced Virginia to him. When I told him she was an ardent fan of his from Brighton, he seemed very pleased. At my suggestion, Virginia extended her scorecard to be autographed. He very obligingly signed his name. He told me he would give me two tickets to the game anytime I wanted them. A gentleman came to talk with him and we went back to our seats.

P.S. Virginia likes his brown eyes. And by the way, the Tigers won from Cleveland's Bob Feller, 4-3.

May 19-Elnora and I went down to the Detroit Leland at Hank's invitation and had lunch with him. We sure had a most enjoyable time, and Hank is the perfect host. It rained off the game so we were unable to use the tickets Hank gave me. We had so much fun at the dinner table. We talked about Hank and the other Tigers, my artwork and home run letters. Hank said that he was puzzled over some way to preserve them. He asked me if I would design his Christmas cards this year. You can bet that I said yes, and I'll do my best to make it something nice. I asked about Buck Newsom and told Hank how he had called me last summer. As a result, Hank gave me some sound advice about Buck and his character. I had already suspected it. He asked about my radio and how the watch ran. When we got to the lobby, he went up to his rooms and soon returned with an autographed photo for each of us plus a handful of candy. Then he took us in his car around town to find a show we wanted to see. He left us in front of the Fox Theatre and went on to the ballpark for another treatment on his back. His car was darling. A gray Lincoln Zephyr coupe with red leather upholstery. We had such a good time. He promised me two tickets to the All Star game if it's played in Detroit next year.

The expensive lapel watch and portable Victor radio given to Marjorie by Hank are still in the possession of the Klein family. The watch still ticks away the correct time. Both the watch and the radio are wonderful mementos, reminding us of years past and the friendship of Marjorie and Hank.

Marjorie Sees Hank One More Time

Nineteen Forty turned out to be an important year for the author. I was farming with my father and at the suggestion of Livingston County Agriculture Extension Agent, S. Ben Thomas, I began attending the Junior Farm Bureau meetings and parties. There, I met many fine young people who had grown up on farms. Some of my early acquaintances in the group were Arza and Chester Clark, Elnora and Frances Sharp, Ld Marshall, August and Virginia Jonckheere, Robert E. Smith, Marjorie Nash, Charles Schultz, Horace Taylor, L.D. Dickerson, and Bernard Kuhns.

One evening in early September, a black Oldsmobile coupe pulled into our driveway. It was Virginia Jonckheere and Marjorie Nash. Inviting them into our house to meet my parents, I soon learned the young ladies were helping to plan a wedding for Marjorie's sister, Elizabeth, and Virginia's brother, August Jonckheere. It would be held in Detroit in October. Virginia was to be a bridesmaid and I was asked to serve as an usher. I gladly accepted and the friendship began.

In November following the wedding, Marjorie and I began to occasionally go together to movies and parties. As Christmas approached, one evening I asked her what she would like for a Christmas gift. "What I would really like is a five-year diary. I used to have one but it's all filled as of the end of last year."

"Thanks for the idea. I'll see if I can find one."

Early in 1941, Marjorie told me she was acquainted with Hank Greenberg but just how well acquainted they were, she never let me know. I thought it was wonderful and told her that I would like to meet Hank. She also told me about the Home Run letters she used to send him and about the radio and watch she had received as Christmas gifts. Marjorie said, "Hank would often give me tickets to attend the Tiger games and usually my seat was in the area behind the dugout where the Tigers wives were seated." She also indicated their friendship was no longer as close as it once had been, but they were still friends. That was good enough for me. "Oh Boy," I thought. Then within a few weeks, I learned she would rather not talk about Hank so I seldom brought up the subject during the following 62 years.

In the new five-year diary in 1941, these four entries stand out as important:

April 29-Wrote letters to Clate, Grandma Nash and Hank Greenberg.

May 6-"Hank's last game" before going to the army, so he ended things with a bang by hitting homers No.1 and No.2, so I sent him two Home Run letters

Hank had learned about the many Jewish people that were disappearing in Hitler's Germany. He began his military service in May of 1941 after appearing in only 19 Tiger games before reporting for duty at Fort Custer. He served through World War II and finally returned to baseball in the summer of 1945.

July 4-Clate and I went to Virginia's wedding. [This was the day when Virginia Jonckheere married Marshall Dayton.]

July 7-Kenneth was here all day. Then he went home with Clate to stay for the summer.

Marjorie is referring to her younger brother, Kenneth Nash. He was an active and ambitious 12-year-old with red hair, anxious to learn and to help with the farm work. He also liked to play baseball.

Marjorie's younger sister Evelyn married Dossie H. Beasley in April of 1941 and a few months later Marjorie and I were making our own wedding plans. We planned to be married at the Grosse Pointe Memorial Presbyterian Church on October 18 of the same year. Both she and I prepared a list of friends and relatives we each would like to send invitations. One day while we were conversing and checking the names on these lists, I casually remarked, "I don't see your friend Hank's name on your list. You are surely going to invite him even though he's at Fort Custer, aren't you?"

"Oh! No! I couldn't do that," she emphatically replied. I failed to ask her why, realizing the topic of Hank was no longer anything she was happy to discuss.

Marjorie and I were married and moved into the house where I was born on the family farm north of Fowlerville. I had taken over the operation of the 230-acre farm from my father early in 1940 and received an agricultural exemption from military service from the Livingston County draft board. My parents had recently moved into the house on their adjoining farm.

Our son Darrell was born on May 24, 1945. The Tigers were again pennant contenders when "Hammerin' Hank" returned from the U.S. Air Force. He had been away from the game more than four years, and was the first major leaguer to return to baseball after the war. In his book, ***The Story of My Life***, Hank writes:

> I spent two weeks getting myself in shape. I had so many blisters from batting practice that skin came off my left hand. The team was on the road, scheduled to return home on July 1. I was taking batting practices and also trying to get my legs in shape. Strangely enough, my legs gave me the most trouble. I had lost a lot of the bounce and speed. As Jimmie Dykes subsequently said, "Greenberg looks like a guy who's running on roller skates." I guess I had slowed down, but in any case the competition wasn't so keen as when I had left.

> In my first game back on July 1, I came out in front of 55,000 people, the largest crowd of the year at Briggs Stadium. Everybody was cheering like mad. After four years in the service, the greeting was nice, but it didn't matter all that much to me. I was just glad to be back alive. I went out there to do my job. I went right back out to left field. We were playing Philadelphia in a double-header and I hit a home run in the eighth inning of the first game. Boy, it felt good to hit that one!

During a series with the Yankees in New York in 1945, Hank met Caral Gimbel. They soon began dating. Then while on the way to spring training in Lakeland, the couple was married in Brunswick, Georgia on February 18, 1946. Caral was the daughter of Bernard Gimbel, the president and principal owner of Gimbel Brothers and Saks Fifth Avenue department stores in New York City.

In August of 1946, Marjorie, my sister Bernice M. Chappel, her husband and I went to a Tigers-Indians game at Briggs Stadium. We arrived early and as we drove around the stadium near the corner of Cherry Street and Michigan Avenue, the attendant stepped out and asked if we were going to the game. We responded affirmatively. He motioned us to turn into the open doorway of the stadium. We were in the Tigers players' parking lot and there was still space for more than a dozen autos behind us. The parking fee was $1.00.

We secured tickets to the game for $1.50 in the lower deck just beyond first base. Hank was playing at first again. Bob Feller was pitching for the Indians and Hal Newhauser for the Tigers. It was a close game, still tied 1-1 in the seventh, when Hank came to bat to open the bottom of the inning for the Tigers. Bob Feller walked Hank and manager Steve O'Neil sent Eddie Mierkowitz in to run for Hank.

The Tigers won the game and the four of us went back to our auto but found several vehicles parked behind us. We would be unable to leave until they moved out of the way. While we sat in the auto waiting, Hank walked by, heading for his Lincoln, parked about 30 feet from us. He opened his door, standing and looking around as he also waited. My dear wife slid down in the seat as soon as she saw him. I asked her, "Please holler at Hank to let him know you are here." I was still hoping to meet him.

"No! No! I don't want him to see me!" she cried as she slid down even farther in the seat. I asked her again. She responded negatively once more, so I decided to walk over to Hank, who was also patiently waiting, and tell him who I was. As I unlocked the door to step out she grabbed my sleeve, "No! No! Please don't!" Clutching my arm tightly in desperation, "I don't want him to know I'm here!"

Finally, after more than 10 minutes, the autos behind us moved and we were able to head home. So another opportunity for me to meet Henry was lost. Will I ever get to meet him? I wondered.

Those Gladiators

In the spring of 1951, Marjorie and I gave up on farming and began a business in Fowlerville. Our son Darrell was then six years old and daughter Debbie arrived in 1954. Darrell was already wild about baseball. He loved to play catch with his dad or his Uncle Kenneth Nash or anyone who came along. He loved to throw or bat stones from the gravel road in front of our house or skip stones across water whenever we were near a lake. He loved to swing a bat and attend Tigers games with us.

Fowlerville High School's Gladiators had some good baseball teams during the early 1960s, and a wonderful coach, Mr. Clem Spillane. In both 1962 and '63, they won the Ingham County League Championship. Darrell's mind was usually on baseball during those years. He also played football until he smashed his left knee. In his final year as a Gladiator, he was named the League's all-star center fielder with a batting average for the season of .550. Other members of the team receiving league all-star honors were second baseman Jon Finlan with a .333 average and LaVerne Nygren, a pitcher who won six games without a loss. Other outstanding members of the 1962 and '63 championship teams were pitchers like Owen Judd and Ken Curtis, shortstop John Munn, Ron Sober, Gordon Hetrick and John Douglass. In mid June of 1963, the Fowlerville team participated in the Capitol City Classic, a tournament where League winning teams from around central Michigan take part. Fowlerville lost in the championship game to Lansing's Sexton High. It was evident that Major League scouts were present during the Classic.

On June 18, 1963 we received a postcard addressed to Darrell from Jack Zeller, General Manager of the Detroit Tigers, inviting Darrell to appear at Briggs Stadium the following Saturday at 10 A.M. to try out with the Tigers. It so happened that Marjorie's niece Ann Jonckheere's wedding to Phil Smith was scheduled at St. Mary's Church in Howell the very same day. Darrell's mother decided that inasmuch as all of the other 19 cousins in the Nash family would be attending, she expected her son to be there. Showing me the card, she said, "We can't let Darrell go to Detroit on Saturday. He would miss Ann's wedding. All of the other cousins will be there and I want him to be there too."

"I think we should let him try out with the Tigers." I responded. "We know he's good at baseball."

"No! I want him to go to the wedding with us."

"What difference does it make if he's not at the wedding?"

"It makes a lot of difference to Mother and me. Ann is Mother's first grandchild to be getting married and she expects all of her grandchildren to be there!"

Darrell had been working part-time in the family business during his high school years. "I think we should show him this postcard as soon as he comes home from work. We could let him drive our auto to Briggs Stadium Saturday morning. He's a good driver."

Darrell Klein in 1963

"No! We cannot do that. We can't let him take our car! We can't let him go! He has to be at the wedding! If the Tigers really want to see him at the Stadium, they will invite him again some other time."

Well, I am not a very good arguer and I don't like to argue. I was thinking that maybe she was right. After all, she has had a lot more experience with the Tigers and Tiger players than I have. Maybe if she thinks so, they will invite him another time. So I reluctantly agreed after she told me she wanted to give Darrell the card herself and explain the reason she expected him to attend the wedding. She also asked me not to mention the situation to Darrell before she had an opportunity to talk with him.

On Saturday morning, the day of the wedding, Marjorie gave the card to Darrell shortly after 8 A.M. This was a heartbreaker for him. He came to me saying, "Why didn't Mom or you give this card to me the day it arrived or at least tell me about it?"

"I'm sorry, son. Your mother asked me not to let you know until we discussed it. Then she wanted to explain to you the reasons she thinks you have to be with us today at the wedding."

"I really wanted to go and try out. Now it's too late. There's no way I could get there by 10 this morning."

"It is pretty late," I replied. "Your mother convinced me that they will probably call you up again some other day."

"OK, I'll call and try to explain." On Saturday morning at about 9:15, he called the Tigers' office. Jack Zeller was not available, so Darrell explained to a secretary, asking her to please let Mr. Zeller know the reason he would not be there. If invited again, he would certainly be there on time.

So, we all attended Ann's wedding and the reception that followed. Everyone except Darrell and I were happy. He well covered his true feelings and no one suspected he was having a problem. As it turned out, the marriage of Ann and Phil lasted only a few months, and Darrell never did get another call from the Tigers, even though he continued to play sandlot baseball until he was nearly 30.

Now, 44 years later, I realize I should have insisted that Darrell go to Briggs Stadium in time for the try-out. This was certainly one of the major mistakes of my life.

The years rolled along. Coach Clem Spillane soon married Ann, Jon Finlan's sister, and moved to Wareham, Massachusetts. One day in July of 2004, I stopped for a brief visit with Jon and was pleasantly surprised to find Clem and Ann there visiting her brother. They were also there to attend the Fowlerville Fair. Jon re-introduced me to Clem, as we had not seen each other in 40 years.

As we were shaking hands, Clem asked, "Are you any relation to Darrell Klein?"

I proudly replied, "Yes, Darrell's my son."

"I've often wondered about him," he said with a grin. "He was such a good baseball player. Good enough to make it into organized baseball. Was he ever called up?"

"Yes," I replied. "This is embarrassing for me to talk about, but the Tigers wanted him to come to the Stadium for a try-out in 1963. On that very day, my wife's niece was to be married and she insisted Darrell just had to attend the wedding. She convinced me that if he was so good, the Tigers would call him up again some other time. Stupidly and to keep peace in the family, I went along with her wishes. Well, even though Darrell called the Tigers office to explain the reason he couldn't make it, he never heard from them again."

"I'm sorry to hear that. He was such a good hitter and fielder! The Dodgers also had their eye on him. Did he ever hear from them?"

"No. I don't think so." Then I went on to explain that Darrell was soon married and had to keep working to earn a living; he was unable to regularly attend college so there was no M.S.U. baseball for Darrell. Later he did find time to take a two-year short course.

Darrell continued to work in the family business and was its General Manager from 1983 to 1997 when it was sold. Very little more was spoken about his baseball days or about his love for baseball until 1995. He and I were on one of our lengthy canoe-camping journeys in Canada's Northwest Territories. This time we were exploring a possible canoe route from Rennie Lake in the headwaters of the Thelon River to Selwyn Lake, in the headwaters of the MacKenzie River. As we sat near our campfire one evening conversing about the beauty of the day, the topic of baseball came up. Darrell said, "I still wish I could have gone to try out with the Tigers. I may not have ever made the team, but perhaps I could have. Of course now I will never know."

"It is a shame I didn't put my foot down and let you know as soon as that card came. I should have insisted you go to try out with them. But I guess I wasn't man enough to argue more. I'm so sorry."

"That's OK." Darrell paused. "I used to think, what a thrill it would be to get out on that field at Briggs Stadium where so many great baseball players had been. Greats like Ty Cobb, Babe Ruth, Charlie Gehringer, Hank Greenberg, Mickey Cochrane, Bob Feller, Lou Gehrig, Ted Williams, and Joe DiMaggio had played. But now I'll never know."

"Yes. It's just too bad. If I had those days to live over again, I would have done things right. You were such a speedy runner. I remember how people called you 'another Fowlerville Flash'—Charlie Gehringer was the original. And how did you ever learn to hit so well? I remember in some of those high school games you would get three or four hits."

"Coach Spillane had a lot to do with that. He taught me to concentrate and think about every pitch coming my way, and to try to hit it out to an open spot in the field where no one could field it. In fact, he had me thinking baseball most all of the time. I was getting poor marks in most of my regular classes and it's likely that I may not have graduated if the coach hadn't pulled some strings for me."

Tribute To Hank Greenberg

Labor Day weekend of 1986 arrived as daughter Debbie and I were paddling and camping along Lake Superior's north shore west of Wawa, Ontario. It was a wonderful few days to be together. We returned home and sometime during the following week, Marjorie casually mentioned, "Hank Greenberg died last week."

"I'm sorry to hear that. How old was he?"

"Seventy-five. I read he died of cancer," she replied.

My brain must have been asleep, as it had been so often down through the years when the topic of Hank came up. I should have reminded her again, how I had always wanted to meet Hank and while discussing him, should have asked why she discontinued her friendship with Hank before we were married. But my lazy brain once more chose to stay relaxed and have no more to say about it.

Marjorie had also saved and stashed away copies of the old newspapers. In the September 5 issue of the *Detroit News*, more than a double-page spread appeared announcing his death and reviewing highlights of Hank's super career. The subtitle of an article written by Joe Falls reads "The Kid from the Bronx didn't let hecklers silence his bat."

Another nearly two-page spread appeared in the September 12 issue of the *Detroit News* under the heading "A Tribute—Fans Remember Hank Greenberg." The opening paragraph reads, "When Hank Greenberg died last week in Beverly Hills, California at age 75, his friends, former teammates, and baseball officials paid tribute. Now it's the fans' turn. Readers responded to our request to share favorite memories of Greenberg, a Hall of Fame slugger who played with the Detroit Tigers for 11 seasons. Here is a small sampling of those letters:

> My earliest memory of Tiger baseball is that famous grand slam home run that Hank Greenberg hit on the last day of the season. That was the day I was infected by Tiger fever. My dad was listening to the game on the radio, and when Greenberg hit that homer,

you would have thought World War II had just ended for the second time, right in our living room. It was joy unlimited. Forty-one years ago, and I have never forgotten it. And I never will. —Doris Applebaum, Oak Park

As a girl of 10 growing up in the Depression years, my dad took me to see the Tigers play at Navin Field. We would sit in the bleachers—so close to Heaven I thought with my child mind. Later in life, I sat in reserved seats with my husband. When I heard them announce his death, memories rushed back to me. Running home from school to hear the games on the radio—hearing the cheering for Hank—seeing him wave to us in the bleachers. I could not help but wonder if he saw the same Heaven I did.

—Anna Marie Bommarito, Harper Woods

When I was 10, Hank was 23. The year was 1934.

There was more to him than homers. He had style and he had class.

He worked hard to be the best on old Frank Gavin's grass.

The bigots came to taunt him because he was a Jew.

He answered them with mighty blows and silenced every boo.

That year, 26 homers were hammered off his bat.

And 63 doubles, who could ask for more than that.

He welcomed eager kids to shag his long fly balls.

He then hit shots into the stands, and bounced balls off the walls.

From out in section 14, we would root for Hankus Pankus.

With one gigantic swing, he used his bat to thank us.

The heroes of a kid go on and on forever.

Will we forget Hank Greenberg? Never, never, never.

—Jack Poole, Warren

As a young boy in the mid 1930s, I still treasure the times my mother drove me down to Navin Field on weekend mornings. We heard that Hank Greenberg came to the park early for batting practice and that management was letting young kids shag fly balls for him. He was bigger than life for me but he taught me an important lesson: practice and be prepared. Another lesson was that the bigger you are, the nicer you can be to those who have not reached fame. He put his country before baseball and his faith before baseball. These are the heroes we want young people to emulate.

—Leonard H. Trunsky, West Bloomfield

Back in the 30s, when I was seven to 10 years old, the YMCA occasionally took us on field trips. One was to Navin Field to see the Tigers play. Hank Greenberg chatted with our group and asked me my name and said, "Harold, I'm going to hit a home run for you today." And he did. I was somewhat chagrined that the field announcer didn't identify that it was for me. Adults at the time suggested that he had told the same thing to half a dozen kids, but I'd rather recall a summer afternoon that Hank Greenberg hit one for me.

— Harold E. Evans, Saginaw

"Rogell to Gehringer to Greenberg." Ty Tyson made those five words one of his WWJ radio broadcasts of Tiger games, because he said them so often. The trio made so many double plays, and Greenberg was the last man in the link. He had to keep one foot on first base, and though the ball often came easy at him, he often had to stretch into the air, or dig it out of the dirt. True, he got the cheers of the crowd, but he always admitted that it was a three-man show. Rogell to Gehringer to Greenberg. Now there are two.

—William T. Rabe, Sault Ste. Marie

As a young teen-ager, I had a tremendous crush on Hank Greenberg. I became an avid baseball fan and since we shared the same last name, my friends called me "Hank." The year 1936 was a leap year in which a female could propose marriage to a male. I sent a written proposal of marriage to Hank. He answered my proposal with a friendly handwritten note to the effect that he wasn't quite ready to marry at the time.

Of course I was thrilled to have a personal note from my hero—never dreaming that anything further would develop. However shortly thereafter, I learned that he was to be a guest speaker at the youth group meeting of Congregation Sharrey Zedek. Of course, I attended so I could meet him in person. I was a very shy 13-year-old, but I found the courage to introduce myself to this gorgeous hunk as the girl who had proposed to him.

With a number of members of the youth group present, he looked at me and with a twinkle in his eyes said, "I accept." I became so flustered that I couldn't say a word and just wanted to melt down to the floor and disappear. It was an unforgettable moment when Hank made a starry-eyed teenager feel very special.

—Harriet (Greenberg) Coleman, Southfield

Jimmy K. was a fifth grader in my Sunday school class in a Presbyterian church years ago. Like most boys of that age, he would rather tease girls, make faces, giggle and generally be obnoxious than listen to the lesson. One morning though, he heard me say something about Jesus being a Jew. He blurted out, "You mean like Hank Greenberg." "Yes," I said. "Oh, Wow!" he replied.

After that, Jimmy was more interested in the Sunday school lessons. I had an easier time teaching, because Hank Greenberg was a Jew. Hank Greenberg would never know how he rated with this little 10-year-old boy. —Lorna Dodd, Ypsilanti

The Mystery Is Solved

The years flew by as the four of us worked in the fertilizer business. Marjorie did artwork and secretarial duties. Our company grew and expanded, operating blend plants in six agricultural communities across lower Michigan. Darrell took over as General Manager in 1983 after working for the company for 23 years. Our daughter Debbie moved on to Michigan State University after spending a couple of years in the family business and is now in her 18th year in the Food Science Department at the former "cow college" in East Lansing, Michigan.

Marjorie and I not only worked together, we also played together, vacationing around our country as well as Mexico, Central America, Canada, and the Caribbean. With Marjorie, work and her family always came first. She was an excellent cook and housekeeper in addition to her work in the business. She sang in our church choir at the Fowlerville United Methodist church. And there was more. Without complaining, she put up with the absence of Darrell, Debbie, and I whenever we decided to go on one of our extended canoe-camping-exploration journeys into Canada's Far North or Alaska.

Those 61 years of my life with Marjorie certainly did fly by until she became ill near Christmas time in 2002. She was such a wonderful wife and mother! But she left us, moving on to Heaven on March 29, 2003. We continue to miss her very much each day.

Three questions popped into my mind as I finished reading the five-year diary in early 2005, questions I now wish that I had asked Marjorie while she was still healthy:

1. The real reason that she and Hank discontinued their friendship.

2. Why she did not want Henry to meet me.

3 The reason that she did not want Darrell to try out with the Tigers.

It was likely we will never know the answers to those questions.

After discussing the diary and the questions with Darrell and Debbie, we agreed that I should try to find the answers. Marjorie's two sisters, Elizabeth and Evelyn, and her brothers, Charles

Robert and Kenneth, were still living. Their parents had already passed on. Was it possible that this had been a long-held family secret? We tried to think of any of Marjorie's friends from those "good old days" who were still alive. We came up with only two, Elnora (Sharp) Munsell and Virginia (Jonckheere) Dayton. I decided that I would try to visit each of them as soon as possible.

On November 9, 2004, I visited Marjorie's sister Evelyn Beasley, who was then residing at American House in Birmingham, Michigan. She had not been well for several months. We had lunch together and as we visited, I told her about recently discovering Marjorie's diary along with gifts and some other mementoes from Hank. I asked her if she had any idea why Marjorie and Henry were no longer friends. "No," she replied, "Let's talk about something else." This was to be my final conversation with Evelyn although I didn't realize it at the time. Evelyn passed away on October 5, 2006.

A few days after my lunch with Evelyn I was welcomed into the home of Elnora Munsell. I had with me the lapel watch engraved on the back "To Marge from Hank," as well as several other gifts Marjorie had received. We conversed for more than an hour. Elnora recalled going to lunch with Hank and Marjorie and attending Tiger games using the tickets he had given her. Elnora said she had no idea why their friendship ended all those years ago, nor was she able to shed any light on either of the other puzzling questions.

Marjorie's second sister Elizabeth died on January 12, 2005. Following her funeral, I discussed the mystery with their brother Kenneth and Elizabeth's son, David Jonckheere. As we chatted I soon asked, "Do either of you have any idea why Marjorie and Hank's friendship came to an end? She never told me." There was no immediate reply.

Then nodding his head with a grin, Ken spoke, "I think I do. I remember the day when Hank came to our house to visit Marjorie. I saw this white Lincoln convertible with the top down driving slowly along our street. As it came closer I could see it was Hank Greenberg. He stopped in front of our house and parked parallel to the sidewalk. I ran to the house, opened the front door and yelled 'Marjorie, Hank Greenberg is here!' I was so excited and happy to see him, guess I hollered a little too loud because even the neighbors heard me. Marjorie must have been in her room upstairs because I heard a lot of noise and footsteps as she hurried down. As soon as Hank came inside, Mother sent me out into the back yard. I was just a lad and I guess she didn't want me listening in."

Marjorie's brothers in 1941
(L) C. Robert Nash
(R) Kenneth H. Nash

"How long did Hank stay?" I asked.

"I don't remember. Guess he wasn't there very long. Dad was at work but then the next morning our father called Marjorie and her two sisters into the living room for a meeting. Dad sat them down on the davenport as Mother and I listened from the kitchen. We heard him say, 'I want you three girls to listen to me and listen good! Yes, Greenberg was here yesterday to visit Marjorie. But enough is enough! I don't want any of you to ever, ever bring a Jew into my house again!' For some reason or other our Dad had no use for Jews," Ken continued, "and I think most of our neighbors felt the same way. Marjorie soon had to break it off with Hank and I was continually reminded that I was not to ever tell anyone about it."

This was the answer to one of my questions. Later when I found time to think about it, what a terrible shock this had to be for my dear wife! She most likely wept on several occasions asking her mother, "What can I do?" Her mother, Laura (Eager) Nash, would have tried to comfort her. Each time they discussed the situation Marjorie's tears would begin to flow and she would likely ask, "What difference does it make, he's such a wonderful man! He's thoughtful and caring and he's so handsome. I know he likes me and I care so much for him. Mother, what difference does it make if he is a Jew?" Her mother would have replied, "I don't think Jews are bad but your father doesn't like them. He has spoken and he is the head of our household. He built our house himself and considers that he owns it. I'm sorry but you have no choice. You will have to let Hank know how your father feels about the situation." Similar discussions between the two of them may have gone on for several days. Marjorie and her mother were close and shared much time together, often shopping at J.L Hudson's or Kern's Department stores in downtown Detroit.

There is no diary entry or exact date noted as to when Marjorie and Hank were last together, however Marjorie kept a framed 8x10 photograph of Hank in his Tigers uniform holding three bats. Handwritten by Hank above his signature were the words, "To Marjorie-My best wishes always." He signed and dated it: Hank Greenberg December 13, 1940. The only other clue is the diary entry of April 29, 1941 stating that she wrote letters to both Hank and Clate on that date.

On March 9, 2005, I visited Virginia Dayton. We had a good conversation and talked about her memories of Hank. She said, "One day Marjorie and I were at a game at Brigg's Stadium. Before the game started, she asked if I would like to meet Hank. I told her 'Of course I would!' 'Come along with me' she replied. I followed her to the front of an empty box opposite first base. When she called to Hank, he came over and she introduced me to him. What a thrill to get to meet him!" Virginia continued, "Then another time I drove to Detroit and picked Marjorie up. We were going to the Tigers game but it was a rainy morning. We heard on the radio the game was postponed. Marjorie phoned up to Hank's room. He invited us both to come up. When we arrived, he welcomed us in. He was still in his pajamas and robe. Later he took us to lunch. She and I went to games together a few times."

Virginia was shocked to learn the reason that Marjorie and Hank's friendship ended. "She never told me what happened. I always wondered but didn't want to ask." She continued, "It must have been that she and her mother decided never to talk about the incident to anyone."

I replied, "Guess they decided to always keep it a secret." While showing Virginia the prospective guest lists for our wedding that Marjorie had kept, I explained how a month before our marriage Marjorie and I were looking over each other's lists and I well remember saying, "I don't see Hank's name on your list. You are certainly going to invite him, aren't you?"

"Oh no! I couldn't do that!" she replied.

To which Virginia said with a grin, "If you had invited Hank, I'm sure he would have been there!"

I asked Virginia if she had any idea why Marjorie did not want Hank to meet me. "No," she replied and paused, "but if her Dad didn't like Hank that may have been the reason."

On April 16 and 17, 2005 I was the guest of Marjorie's older brother C. Robert and his wife Ann Nash in Richland, Washington. They entertained me royally including a gathering of their nearby family. When I queried Robert about the reason Marjorie's friendship with Hank ended, he did not give a direct answer but replied, "You should have heard our father when he learned that Marjorie was beginning to go on dates with you, after he learned your name was spelled K-L-E-I-N!" With an expression of disgust on his face, Robert pounded his fist on the table and with a raised voice, imitating his father talking to Marjorie, said, "Now don't tell me you have found another Damned Jew!" Robert continued, "It took a few weeks before mother and Marjorie convinced our father that you were of English and German descent and really not the Jew he thought you were."

I replied with a smile, "My name is the Jewish spelling. It is possible that I may have a trace of Jewish blood in my veins from many generations ago, and if so, I'm proud of it."

Thus I finally realized the reason Marjorie had preferred not to tell me about Hank Greenberg. She did not want me to know her father's true feelings about Jews. She most likely thought, 'If Clate ever learned about why I had to give up on Hank, he would think much less of my father.' So now I have the answer to most of my questions. Actually, I should thank her father, Maurice J. Nash, and if possible would have done so, for ending Marjorie and Hank's friendship. Otherwise, I may never have had the opportunity to meet and enjoy having Marjorie as my loving wife for so many years.

Rapid Robert Feller

While planning this manuscript, I felt a need to find former Big League players who had been acquainted with Hank Greenberg. Following his playing days with the Tigers and Pittsburgh Pirates, Hank ran the farm system of the Cleveland Indians for his friend, Bill Veeck, for a couple of years. Then he spent five years as the Tribes' General Manager. These were the years 1948 to 1954, while Bob Feller was still pitching for the Indians.

I well remember the dozens of occasions when Bob Feller had left Hank standing at the plate following the third strike. Consequently, I decided to try to get in touch with Mr. Feller. In February of 2006 I mailed him a letter of introduction at Chain of Lakes Park in Winter Haven, Florida, the spring training home of the Cleveland Indians. This letter was about our finding Marjorie's five-year diary in which he was frequently mentioned and her passion for Hank Greenberg. Included in the letter was my request that we meet for a few minutes before the Indians/Tigers game on March 4.

Knowing he was one of baseball's all-time greatest pitchers, prior to driving to Florida, I checked the Internet to learn more about him. The Baseball Historian says, "Bob Feller became a legend in his time. His rapid fastball was considered faster than that of anyone else in the history of the game. Cleveland Indians' Manager Steve O'Neill remembered, 'Rapid Robert's first appearance was in Cleveland's old League Park. Playing in an exhibition game against the St. Louis Cardinals, O'Neill, a former catcher, decided to catch Feller personally and have him pitch the middle three innings. The first batter was thrown out trying to bunt. Feller's other eight outs were all strikeouts. Cardinals' hitter, Leo Durocher, took two strikes and threw his bat on the ground. Durocher roared, 'This kid looks at third base and stuffs the ball down your throat.'"

Robert William Andrew Feller was born on November 3, 1918 near Van Meter, Iowa. He was taught to pitch by his father, an Iowa farmer who built a diamond on the farm for his son in 1932. He was signed at age 16 to play for Cleveland for $1.00 by scout Cy Slapnicka. He also received a baseball autographed by all of the Indians.

There is a Bob Feller Museum in Van Meter, Iowa, built in 1998 and designed by Feller's son Stephen. From there come several other interesting facts about 'Rapid Robert':

- By the time he enlisted at age 22, Bob Feller had become the first pitcher in Major League history to win 20 or more games before the age of 21 and had 109 Major League victories. This is by far the most victories ever recorded in the Major Leagues by a 22-year-old pitcher.
- On Opening Day in Chicago 1940, Bob Feller pitched his first of three no-hitters, the only no-hitter pitched on Opening Day in Major League history.
- Bob Feller led the American League in victories for six seasons during his career. Overall, he won 266 games while losing only 162. Only the four years spent in military service prevented him from winning more than 300 games, while compiling 2,581 strikeouts. Those four years, in all probability, cost him at least 100 victories as well as establishing other pitching records that would have stood for decades.
- Bob Feller – Cleveland Indians' pitcher (1936-1956) – was elected into Baseball's Hall of Fame in January of 1962 and was inducted into the Hall in July of the same year.
- In July of 1969, he was selected as the "Greatest Living Right-Hand Pitcher" as part of Professional Baseball's Centennial Celebration.
- He was the winningest pitcher in Cleveland Indians' History.
- He led the American League in strikeouts seven times.

In his first Major League start against the St. Louis Browns, Bob Feller fanned 15 hitters and never looked back. For twenty years, all with the Indians, this teenage phenomenon dominated American League batters with his blazing fastball and bending curve. He hurled three no-hitters, including the only Opening Day gem, notched 12 one-hitters, served in World War II, and won 19 games for Cleveland's 1948 World Championship team, according to The Baseball Page. It also says his best season was in 1940, when Feller opened the season with a no-hitter on April 16 in Comiskey Park, in 47-degree weather. On the final day of the season, he lost 2-0 to Detroit, as the Tigers clinched the pennant. Between those two starts, he was masterful. He went 27-11 with a 2.61 Earned Run Average and 261 Strikeouts in more than 320 innings. He completed 31 of his 37 starts and had four saves. He surrendered just 13 home runs.

Bob Feller was a war hero in World War II. He enlisted in the U.S. Navy on December 8, 1941, the day after Pearl Harbor. He immediately volunteered for combat service, becoming the chief of an anti-aircraft gun crew on the *USS Alabama*. He lost almost four baseball seasons to military duty but was still at the top of his game when he returned. In his first year back from the war, he set a new record for strikeouts in a season. Three hundred and forty-eight in 1946. While in the Navy, he earned five campaign ribbons and eight battle stars.

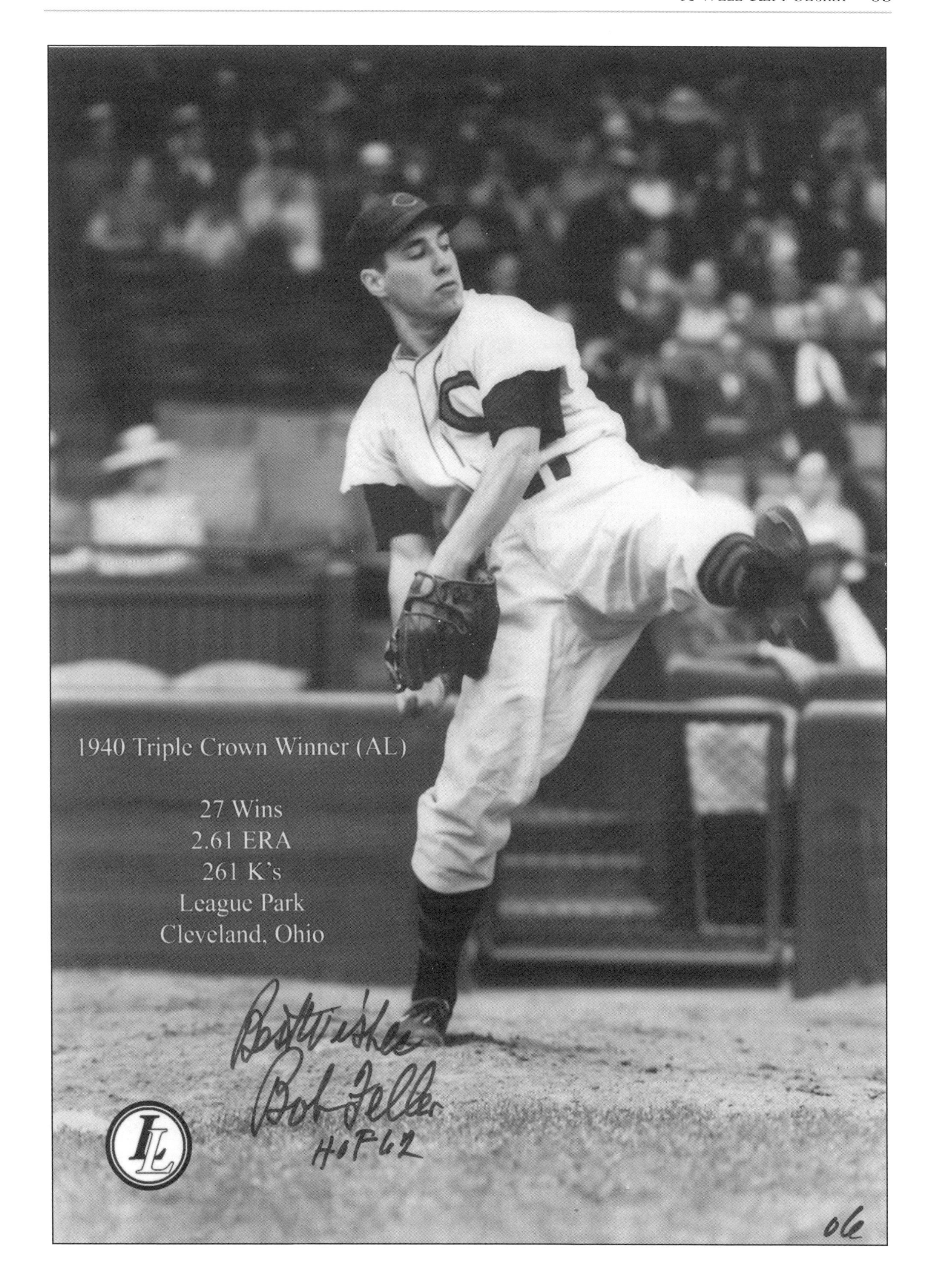
1940 Triple Crown Winner (AL)
27 Wins
2.61 ERA
261 K's
League Park
Cleveland, Ohio
Best Wishes
Bob Feller
HOF 62
IL
06

Arriving at the ballpark early on March 4, I did get to meet the Hall of Famer before the game. He was very busy meeting Indians' fans who lined up to shake his hand and get his autograph. He was expecting me. One of the first things he said when we met was, "I am constantly bothered by people who are writing a book. I turn them all down. You know time is money and there is no money in writing!" I nodded my head in agreement. Bob then glanced at the line of fans waiting for him and continued, "But in your case, I could spare a half hour or so at my convenience. I'm going to do this for you because you and I are about the same age. You can call me at my hotel and we'll try to find some time near the middle of next week," he autographed a photo and gave it to me. The line of other people standing and waiting was getting longer, so I moved on to watch the baseball game.

A few minutes before game time, Mr. Feller appeared on the field near the dugout and eased a few pitches to a catcher. He often throws out the opening pitch at home games in Winter Haven. Following the singing of the National Anthem, the P.A. system announcer introduced 'The Cleveland Indians Hall of Fame Pitcher, Mr. Rapid Robert Feller,' to which the 3,000-plus fans in the stands loudly cheered. Robert doffed his cap, taking bows before walking back into the dugout. Someone else threw out the opening pitch. The Indians won from the Tigers 5-3.

On the following Tuesday, the two of us met again. Bob Feller welcomed me into his cozy hotel rooms near the ballpark. We discussed his baseball playing days, both Marjorie and Hank and various other baseball topics. I briefly explained the five-year diary and told Bob, "The morning after Hank had hit his 57th and 58th home runs, he told Marjorie he would try his darndest to get numbers 59 and 60 in the remaining five games of the season."

"Yes," Bob grinned. "Four of those final games were played in Cleveland and he didn't get another homer. I pitched the first game of a double-header on the last day of the season. I was going along pretty good. Then in the seventh inning, Hank doubled off the left field wall, ruining my chance for another no-hitter. Hank did strike out the other times he came to the plate." Then he added, "There were sports writers there from all over the country, thinking that Hank might still tie Babe Ruth's record of 60. But he didn't make it!"

"Wasn't that the same game that you struck out 18 batters?"

"Yes," he replied with a grin. "I don't like to brag, but you probably know that when I was 17 years old, I broke the American League record with 17 strike-outs in a single game against Philadelphia Athletics and that tied Dizzy Dean's National League record. But in this game, I was lucky again. I struck out 18 batters. One of the Tigers, Chet Laabs, actually fanned five times in the game. The only thing that victory did for me was to make me the Major League's Strike-out King for a single game."

"Who were the toughest batters you faced during your 20 years with the Indians?"

"Tommy Heinrich, Taft Wright, and Rip Radcliff," he replied. "They were all fast ball hitters."

I began to show Bob samples of the Home Run Letters Marjorie used to send Hank and letters he had mailed to her. Robert stopped me saying, "Put them away. I've seen enough." However, he looked closely at the lapel watch, reading the engraving, 'To Marge from Hank.'

A brief pause and Bob continued, "Hank became our General Manager, taking over from Bill Veeck. Hank's sons became friends with my sons and they attended private school together. Hank's number came up early before World War II and he was drafted. Not a volunteer. And Hank's wife Caral didn't like Cleveland. She refused to live there. But her father, Mr. Gimbel, really liked Hank and baseball much better than Caral did." Still reminiscing, Bob went on to say, "I met Hank one time during the war while I was on shore leave in Hong Kong. I noticed this tall guy standing head and shoulders above the mass of people on the street and there was Hank. We were mighty happy to see each other."

I asked Bob about Charlie Gehringer. "He was from my home town of Fowlerville. Some of his relatives are still living in our area."

He replied, "He was a real good man and a great baseball player. A quiet guy who never said much and was always in the right place at the right time. Charlie was what we called a guess hitter. He guessed right a lot because his lifetime average was about .320. I saw Charlie play in the 1934 World Series when the Tigers lost to the Cardinals in seven games. I well remember his power at the plate and at second base. He was highly thought of by everyone in baseball. He was a gentleman and a great second baseman."

I told Bob how surprised I was to learn just how busy he was when we met on Saturday at the ballpark. "Most guys who are anywhere near our age have really slowed down."

"Well I have to have something to do," he replied, "and I still enjoy baseball."

Thanking Bob for his time and information, he suggested I might like to read his *Little Black Book of Baseball Wisdom.* Then, giving me his home address and phone number, he said, "If you have other questions or need more information be sure to let me know and I'll get back to you." We said goodbye.

On a Sunday evening in June 2006, I watched 'War Stories' with Oliver North. The show was about American battles in the Pacific. The special guest was Robert Feller. He was introduced as a hero of World War II, to which he replied, "Real Heroes don't come back from Wars." He said, "I joined the Navy to win the war and I was there to help do it." He was a captain of a battery of the big guns on the *USS Alabama*, and he said, "In the battle for Siapan we leveled the Japanese Air Force, and then we were in more heavy action in the Philippine Sea."

Former Major League baseball players had this to say about Bob:

> "The fastest and best pitcher I ever saw during my career was Bob Feller. He had the best fastball and curve I've ever seen." ***—Hall of Famer, Ted Williams***

> "It wasn't until you hit against him that you knew how fast he really was, until you saw with your own eyes that ball jumping at you." ***—Hall of Famer, Ted Lyons***

> "I hit Bob Feller halfway decent, but golly, it was tough. He'd curve you 3-0 and 3-1, and that's not in the Bible." ***—Hall of Famer, Charlie Gehringer***

> "When you talk about great pitching, Lefty Grove and Bob Feller were outstanding. They were by far the two best pitchers during my era. Both of them had tremendous fastballs and Feller had a fantastic curve ball that was almost unhittable if you were a right-handed batter. He was also a little wild so you had a little respect for him. As for a right-handed pitcher, Bob Feller was in a class by himself." ***—Hall of Famer, Hank Greenberg***

The Fowlerville Flash

Charles Leonard Gehringer was born on a farm near Fowlerville, Michigan on May 11, 1903. Charlie played his entire career, 19 seasons, with the Detroit Tigers, from 1924 through 1942. He batted left-handed and threw right-handed. He has been considered by many to be the greatest second baseman of all time.

Charlie Gehringer was often called 'The Fowlerville Flash.' He covered second base in a smooth, seemingly effortless style. He had quick hands and rarely lost any ball he got his glove on. Gehringer led all American League second basemen in fielding percentage nine times, led or tied for the lead in assists seven times, and had the most putouts three times. Baseball authority H.G. Salsinger wrote about Charlie, "He lacks showmanship, but he has polish that no other second baseman, with the exception of the great Napoleon Lajole, ever had. He was so well schooled himself in the technique of his position that he makes the most difficult plays look easy."

He was also called 'The Mechanical Man.' "You wind him up Opening Day and forget him," teammate Doc Cramer once said. Detroit manager Mickey Cochrane explained, "Charlie says 'hello' on Opening Day, 'goodbye' on Closing Day, and in between hits .350." His silence and lack of color were legendary. During a game in the 1930s, Detroit shortstop Bill Rogell captured a windblown pop fly well on the second-base side of the infield and accidentally spiked Gehringer. "I can catch those too," Gehringer said mildly and limped back to his position.

Following one year at the University of Michigan, the Tigers signed Gehringer in 1924 on the recommendation of former Tiger star Bobby Veach. The legend persists that then manager Ty Cobb doubted the slim youngster's ability to hit Major League pitching. Cobb later said, "I knew Charlie would hit and I was so anxious to sign him that I didn't even take the time to change out of my uniform before rushing him into the front office to sign a contract." In 1926, Gehringer became the Tigers' regular second baseman.

A reliable hitter with good power, Charlie led the American League in batting in 1937 with a .371 mark. He was chosen Most Valuable Player that season. He had more than 200 hits in seven different seasons and led the league in hits and runs scored in 1929 and again in 1934. He led once in triples and twice in doubles, ranking tenth all-time in two-base hits. Seven times he had more than 100 Runs Batted In. In 1929, he topped the American League in stolen bases. His controlled, left-handed batting swing made him difficult to strike out. In 16 full seasons, his strikeouts ranged from 16 to 42.

Gehringer starred for Tigers pennant winners in 1934, 1935 and 1940. He slumped in 1942, and then entered the Navy for three years. From 1951 through 1953, he served as Detroit's general manager and vice president, continuing in the latter position through 1959. At the time of baseball's centennial celebration in 1969, a special committee of baseball writers named him the game's greatest living second baseman.

After his retirement, Charlie coached for Detroit, served as club executive, and as a member of the Baseball Hall of Fame Committee of Veterans (1953-1990). Gehringer was voted into the Baseball Hall of Fame in 1949. The Tigers retired his uniform number 2 in a 1983 ceremony at Tiger Stadium, along with the number 5 of former teammate Hank Greenberg. Both players were on hand for the ceremony. In 1999, Gehringer ranked number 46 on the *Sporting News* list of the 100 Greatest Baseball Players, and was nominated as a finalist for the Major League Baseball All-Century Team.

In research for this narrative, I found a wonderful book written by Richard Bak called ***Cobb Would Have Caught It*: *The Golden Age of Baseball in Detroit***, which Wayne State University published in 1991. Chapter nine of the book consists of a lengthy interview with Charlie Gehringer at his then home in the Detroit suburb of Beverly Hills in 1982. Following are excerpts from the Richard Bak interview as Charlie speaks of his baseball career:

> I think it was Lefty Gomez of the Yankees who gave me the 'Mechanical Man' name. He made the statement to the papers once that 'You wind Gehringer up in the spring and turn him off in the fall and in between he hits .340.' Unfortunately it's not quite that easy. Like anything, it's a lot of hard work and practice.
>
> Looking back, I'd have to say that starting in pro ball was plain luck. I grew up on a farm outside Fowlerville. It was a big farm, 15 cattle and about 230 acres, and it took two or three people to keep it going. My parents had a feeling that I wasn't going to like it on the farm. My older brother (George) was doing most of the heavy work, driving the tractor and running the heavy equipment. My dad (Leonard Gehringer) was still alive and we had a hired man too so it gave me a chance to go away to college for a year. I had an idea that I'd like to be in sports, maybe coaching. I took phys ed classes at the University of Michigan (after graduating from Fowlerville High School in 1922), I went with more or less a baseball background, but I went out for football. I remember Ray Fisher, who was coaching baseball then, caught me on the sidelines one day at practice. 'Don't get too excited about this game,' he said. 'Don't worry.' I said, 'I won't.'
>
> Funny thing is, I won a letter in basketball but didn't get one in baseball. I'd pitched all through high school. Just lost one game. That was 2-1 to Detroit Northern, who always played us in a double-header whenever they came out to play Howell, the next little town. I pitched a little bit in pro ball, but after they started knocking me around pretty

good I said, 'Well, there must be a difference.' So I decided to try second base. I always could hit pretty good.

We used to have a super fan back home (Floyd Smith) who hunted with Bobby Veach, the old Tiger outfielder. He asked Veach if it was all right for me to go down to Detroit for a workout. Today, of course, you couldn't hide a prospect if you wanted to. But this was 1923, and it was possible to get a tryout with a Major League club fairly easy, providing you had some potential. They didn't want you cluttering up the field. So I went down for about a week in the fall of the year. Ty Cobb was the manager then, and apparently, he was so impressed he went up in his uniform to Mr. Navin, the club owner, and got him out of his office to take a look at me. I signed a contract with the Tigers and I can't remember if I got a bonus. Maybe five hundred dollars. But I would've signed for nothing.

When I was a kid, you see, I used to keep a kind of scrapbook. I used to paste newspaper pictures of Cobb and Veach and Harry Heilmann, and here I was going to play with them. I lived with a family from Fowlerville my first couple of years. Lived in a great neighborhood at that time, but it's deteriorated a little since: Twelfth and Pingree Street. Gee, there were some nice little bungalows. Think I paid ten dollars a week and got good food and lodging.

Second jobs? I think you had to have one. Very few players stayed here during the winter. Most of them were from the south in those days and they were all pretty much small town kids. I think they all went back home after the season. Of course, you always had guys who liked to hunt and fish. I didn't care too much for hunting. I never had a gun, and I could never have shot anything if I'd had one. I always said I'd never shoot anything unless it chased me, and so far that hasn't happened.

In the off-season, I'd work at J.L. Hudson's during the holidays. I enjoyed that, gave me something to do, and I met a lot of nice people. I used to take the Trumbull streetcar down.

Didn't have a car in those days, so I always jumped on the streetcar and went downtown. Seems like that was the way everybody was going. Good service. At least we didn't know any better. I used to even take the Trumbull streetcar and go back out after a ball game. If you had a bad day, though, you had to put some plugs in your ears. The fans were getting on the same car and you'd hear about it. They'd say, 'Who was that turkey out there playing today?'

I used to go on barnstorming tours every year. At that time you didn't have television, so people were curious to see Major Leaguers play ball. Out West, up North, through the Dakotas...We went through Canada one year. We used to draw a lot of people and have a lot of fun. We'd have a good club, Bill Dickey, Heinie Manush, George Uhle, and play local teams or another club that traveled with us.

Most of those little town teams didn't give you much trouble, but those colored teams would. I traveled one year with Satchel Paige and his group of colored boys from Chicago. We went up through the Dakotas and Minnesota and Kansas. Got to bat against Satchel every other day, which wasn't much fun. He could throw that fastball! He also had his hesitation pitch where he'd step forward, hang onto the ball for a second, then let it float up there. Kind of a change of pace. Satchel pitched almost every game. He'd generally start and pitch about three innings. Everybody wanted to see him pitch, so he had to. He was a clown.

Ty Cobb was a hateful guy, I think he wanted it that way; felt it made him a better player. I never heard him say anything good about anybody. He died a pretty bitter man. I think he had so many regrets it made him pretty miserable. Nobody liked him as a manager. He was such a great player himself, he figured that if he told you something, there was no reason why you couldn't do it as well as he did. But a lot of guys don't have that ability. He couldn't understand that. Cobb was jealous of everybody and a strict disciplinarian. He had very few friends. All players shrunk away from him, especially the pitchers. Golly, he wore a path from center field to the pitcher's mound. When he relieved a pitcher, he'd just grab that ball away from him.

But he was super for the first couple years I was up. Golly, he was like a father to me. He took care of me, coached me, rode with me on the train and all that. He even made me use his own bat, which was kind of a thin little thing. I said, 'Gee, I'd like a little more batting space,' but I didn't dare use another one. He would've shipped me to Siberia. He was a hard fellow to figure, to say the least. I played parts of three seasons with Cobb as manager. Cobb played a few games and did fairly well. He'd have been all right if they'd had the designated hitter back then, because at that time Cobb couldn't field or run. It was pretty hard to use him in a crucial spot. He was still intimidating though. I remember in the fall, when the rosters got bigger and rookies came into town, Cobb would sit on the bench with a file, sharpening his spikes. In the old days, you had to go through our dugout to get to the visitors' dugout. All these kids would get the message. Their eyes would bulge out a little. Of course, at that time Cobb was over the hill and he didn't play much. But he'd still cut you to pieces if you got in his way, and they all realized that.

Yeah, he had a super career. He made a lot of money. I guess he got to know some of the people here who gave him some good tips. I remember when I first came along as a kid, making four thousand dollars a year, and he was telling me to buy General Motors and Coca Cola stock. Which was good advice. But you had to live too, besides buying stock.

My first full season was 1926, Cobb's last season in Detroit. For the next several years we generally had a heavy-hitting ball club, but we couldn't win anything because of our pitching. When I first came up we had Heilmann, Cobb and Veach in the outfield, and guys like Heinie Manush and Bob Fothergill sitting on the bench, even though they were hitting .350. Now, when you see kids hitting .240 playing regularly, it's laughable.

Harry Heilmann was another super guy. He played a little first base, but mostly right field. He was a good fielder with a good throwing arm, but he was slow and couldn't cover a lot of ground. But he sure could hit. Seemed like every other year he'd win the batting championship. He'd hit .390, .395, and over .400 one year. A tremendous hitter. Cobb couldn't hit any better than that, so he didn't fool with him. Besides, Heilmann was so big and strong I don't think Cobb would get very nasty with him.

I don't know why the averages were so much higher then. Golly, the pitchers back then used to cheat, used to keep the ball in play forever. It'd get so black you could hardly see it. They threw a lot of spitballs, knuckle balls...You talk to a modern ball player, and he thinks the pitching must've been horrible with the averages we compiled. But it really wasn't. You saw Lefty Grove and Bob Feller and Red Ruffing—they were no picnic. I hit Feller halfway decent, but golly, it was tough. He'd curve you 3-0 and 3-1, and that's not in the Bible. He was just wild enough so you had to be kind of loose and easy up there.

Cobb left after 1926 and played his last couple of years with Philadelphia. George Moriarty took over as manager and he hated Cobb's guts. He'd sit in the dugout and call Cobb every name in the book as he ran to first. Cobb would hear, of course, but Moriarty was one guy he'd never challenge because Moriarty was a tough cookie. Ordinarily, if the guy was smaller or less able to defend himself, Cobb would've come over and cleaned the bench out, I guess.

Bucky Harris came over from Washington to manage in 1929. Bucky was a little too nice. He was a super guy to play with. Wouldn't scream at anyone. Not like Cochrane. He'd get you and let you know what the score was. I suppose you've got to be tough in a way, because you've got all kinds of guys to handle. But I never heard Bucky Harris second guess anyone. The fact that he was so easy to play for probably didn't help his managing, but you'd never want to work for a nicer guy.

Mickey Cochrane turned it all around in 1934. We were that close and needed a catcher badly.

We got Cochrane from Philadelphia and then we got Goose Goslin from Washington; in both cases it worked out well. Mickey was a super guy and we needed him so badly, what with these young pitchers we had coming along, like Schoolboy Rowe and Tommy Bridges. It was like getting a good quarterback in football. You're dead without one, and it's the same way with a catcher.

Tommy Bridges? I was always glad that he was on our side. A super little pitcher. In fact, I'd have to say he was as good as Hal Newhauser. Maybe his record wasn't as good, but he had some great years.

He had probably the best curve ball I ever stood behind. I've seen him throw that curve ball at a guy's head, and the batter would fall flat on his rear end thinking it was going to hit him, and then the ball would go over the plate for a strike. You think he didn't make the batter look silly?

Billy Rogell came over from the Red Sox in 1930 and he left in '39. Those 10 years were fine. Got along great. Before that I'd played with something like 22 different shortstops. It was fantastic the way they were coming and going. I don't think anyone stayed a year until Rogell came. Rogell and Cochrane were two of a kind—they were both a little short-fused. I'll say one thing about Billy: I don't think I ever got to the ballpark but where he wasn't already there. I don't care how early I got there, he was always ahead of me. That's how eager he was to operate. He was a real nut for baseball.

I had a reputation for always taking the first pitch, but that was only partly true. I hit a lot with men on base. But against the average pitcher, I thought I was a better hitter with two strikes. Many times you go up there and think, well, I've got two or three more pitches, and you get careless. You swing at bad balls and make an out. With two strikes you concentrate more, you cut down on your swing and put the ball in play.

We had very few run-ins with umpires in my day, I never got thrown out of a game. I could never understand what an umpire's ancestry had to do with a call, anyway. I felt you had to be friendly with them or you're not going to get the best of it. I would never turn around and tell them that they did this or that wrong. If I wanted to say something to them, I'd say it out of the corner of my mouth or look the other direction. Try showing them up, and you'll be in the showers.

We played the Cardinals in the '34 World Series. To this day I think Brick Owens, the umpire, beat us out of the championship. We had St. Louis down, three games to two, and we should've won the sixth game. Late in the game, Owens called Cochrane out on a play at third even though all of the photographs show that he was safe by a mile. We wound up losing to Paul Dean by a run. Had Cochrane been called safe on that play, we would've had the bases loaded with nobody out and we could've had a big inning. Then in game seven, Dizzy Dean shut us out, 11-0, and that was that.

We won again in 1935, even though we were in sixth place as late as May. We played the Cubs, and Hank Greenberg got hurt in that series. Hank, of course, was our big gun. A strong guy. He had long arms and a big arc to his swing, so even if he was fooled on a pitch he could still hit the ball a long ways.

His famous saying to me was, 'Just get the runner over to third.' Hank loved those RBIs. He had 183 one season. Just get 'em over to third, so Hank could drive 'em in. I told him once, 'You'd trip a runner coming around third base just so you could knock him in yourself.'

But winning the first World Series was a big thrill. The entire town was ga-ga. I tried to take a friend downtown, but golly, everything was blocked up. You couldn't cross the streets, the city was such a mess. First world championship for Detroit. Seemed like everybody was downtown, whoopin' and hollerin'.

Rudy York came up a year or two later. He came up as a catcher, but he wasn't very good. They tried him at third, and he was even worse there. They finally moved Greenberg to left field and put Rudy at first base. They had to find some place for Rudy because he was such a good hitter. I roomed with Rudy for about a year. He used to like to drink his beer, and he'd smoke cigarettes when he went to bed. If the cigarette burned his fingers, then he'd wake up and put it out. But quite often he'd fall asleep and then he'd drop that burning cigarette. I don't know how many mattresses he burned up. We always said he led the league in burned mattresses. I finally moved in with someone else. I wanted a little better chance of getting out in case he burned the hotel down.

But I liked the baseball life. We traveled by train; two private coaches along with a diner on the back. The food was super and we'd play bridge, pinochle, and hearts en route. We all had our own berths; no upper deckers. I'd prefer to travel that way than fly.

I was the on-deck hitter when (Mickey) Cochrane got hit by Bump Hadley in Yankee Stadium. My goodness, he went down like someone had hit him with an ax. He got hit right above the ear. The ball bounced right back to the pitcher. Some doctor said that if it'd been an inch lower he probably would never have awakened. He later tried managing from the bench, but I think he had too much time to think on the bench. He'd outguess himself. On the field he was able to make instantaneous decisions. Whether the beaning had any effect on it, I don't know.

Mr Navin died the winter after we won the World Series and Mr. Briggs, who had been a silent partner, took over. He fired Mickey halfway through the '38 season. You would have thought that somebody with Mickey's record would find a place in the Tigers' organization. Of course, Mickey was pretty quick on the draw with his temper, as was Briggs and I guess Briggs and Cochrane had a word fest that didn't help matters. Del Baker replaced Cochrane. He was the last manager I played for. I liked to play for him. He was all baseball, morning, noon, and night. He was pretty experienced. He'd never played much Major League ball, but he was connected with it all his life.

We surprised a lot of people, including ourselves, when we won the pennant in 1940. The Yankees had won four straight World Series, and most of our team was over the hill. Cleveland had such a great team. We nosed them out in the last series of the year. They thought they had it all wrapped up until the last couple weeks of the season, when everything fell apart over there.

We kept up our stats then, but not like they do today. I don't think anybody thought about getting 3000 hits in those days. In fact, the Hall of Fame wasn't even around till I was finishing up, so you didn't give that much consideration. As it turned out, I needed just a few more hits to reach 3000. I might've gotten them if I didn't have to go in the service in World War II. After Pearl Harbor, I signed up for the draft. But instead of waiting to get drafted, I enlisted in the Navy. I was 38 at the time, and I wasn't about to go in as a foot soldier at that age. I thought I'd get into something better.

We had enough training to do as it was. But I enjoyed it. In fact, I came out of the service in such good shape that I felt I could've played a few more years. But we had a good business going by that time, so I said what the heck. We were selling fabrics to auto manufacturers. I started that in '38, so when I came back in '45 it was really going good. Rather than get involved in baseball again and more or less start over with new management, I decided to stick with what I got. So I retired.

The most I ever made? About $40,000. I probably got more than anyone on the club with the exception of Greenberg. I think Hank got a little more. Of course, you have to think that in those days you could buy a brand new Cadillac for $2000. In fact, I bought my first house in Detroit, a brand new place on Grand River out near Rosedale Park, for $10,500 in 1934. It was a nice house, never even lived in. It was built by a builder whose wife died the week he finished it. After my father died my mother (Teresa Gehringer) was up on the farm pretty much by herself, so I moved her in. She was a diabetic and needed someone to look after her. I might've married sooner than I did but I couldn't see bringing a wife into that kind of situation. But she was a great fan. She'd come out to the ballpark or listen to the games out on the porch.

My greatest thrill? You know, people ask me that all the time, and I've got to say that every day in the Major Leagues is a thrill, and the next game is even bigger. Still, one that I'll always remember is back in 1929 when the folks from my home town of Fowlerville had a day for me at Navin Field. They presented me with a set of golf clubs. They were beautiful; matched Spalding irons and woods with a beautiful leather bag. They also were right-handed and of course I'm left-handed. But I learned how to play the game right-handed, those clubs were so nice. Anyway, we played the Yankees that day and we won big. I started off with a home run. I had four hits and almost hit for the cycle, and to top it off I stole home. I probably had some better afternoons but that was kind of a special day.

Charlie Gehringer played every inning of the first six All-Star Games as starting second baseman for the American League, batting a record .500 in 20 Mid-Summer Classic at-bats.

Charlie died in January 1993 in Bloomfield Hills, Michigan at age 89.

In More Recent Years

To bring this 'Well-Kept Secret' to a conclusion, let us look briefly at a few highlights of the Detroit Tiger teams following their Glory Days. The next outstanding year was 1961 when they won 101 games. Unfortunately, they still finished eight games behind the Yankees, one of the few times a team had failed to reach the post season despite winning over 100 games. First baseman Norm Cash had the best batting average in the American League: a remarkably high .361. He never hit over .286 before or after the '61 season.

Outfielder Al Kaline burst onto the scene in Detroit, winning the batting crown in 1955 at age 20—the youngest player ever to do so. He would hit over .300 eight times in his career, and featured one of the league's best arms in right field. Pitchers Mickey Lolich and Denny McLain would also enter the rotation during the middle of the decade. As this winning nucleus developed, they would repeatedly post winning records throughout the 1960s. Mayo Smith took over as manager in 1967 and the team was eliminated on the final day of the season, setting the stage for their historic 1968 campaign.

The 1968 title, which occurred one year after the 12th Street riot ravaged Detroit, helped to heal citywide tensions. The Tigers easily won the American League with many dramatic, come-from-behind victories during the regular season. In the "Year of the Pitcher," the controversial Denny McLain became the first pitcher since Dizzy Dean in 1934 to win 30 games, finishing with a 31-6 record.

In game one of the 1968 World Series, ace Bob Gibson struck out a World Series record 17 Tigers in a 4-0 shutout. The Tiger bats won the day in the second game in St. Louis. Mickey Lolich held St. Louis to a single run on six hits and added a home run in his own cause. The Tigers lost badly in games three and four at Tiger Stadium, 7-3 and 10-1. In game four, some accounts accused Tigers manager Mayo Smith of stalling in hopes that an approaching storm would wash out the game. With their backs against the wall, Lolich took the mound again in game five. The Tigers were eight outs away from elimination before a two-run single from Al Kaline and another RBI by Norm Cash gave Detroit a 5-3 lead they would not relinquish. As the series returned to St. Louis,

McLain pitched on two days' rest. Any concerns about the Tigers' ace having a sore arm were quickly eliminated. The Tigers scored 10 runs in the third inning, including a grand slam from Jim Northrup, in a 13-1 laugher. The deciding game seven pitted Lolich, pitching on two days rest, against Gibson. The Tigers struck first with a Jim Northrup triple, scoring Cash and Willie Horton to give the visitors a 2-0 lead. Catcher Bill Freehan added a double to give Lolich a 3-0 lead with nine outs to go. Don Wert's RBI single in the ninth added an insurance run, and a ninth-inning solo shot from Mike Shannon of St. Louis was the Cards' only response. Tim McCarver, the next batter, popped up to Freehan in foul territory and the Tigers were champions of baseball again.

Then in 1976, Tigers fans received a glimmer of hope when rookie phenom Mark Fidrych made his debut. Fidrych, known as "The Bird," was a crazy character known for talking to the baseball. During a game against the Yankees, Graig Nettles responded to Fidrych's antics by talking to his bat. After making an out, he later lamented that his Japanese-made bat did not understand him. Fidrych was the starting pitcher for the American League in the All Star Game played that year in Philadelphia to celebrate the American Bicentennial. He finished the season with a record of 19-9 and an American League-leading ERA of 2.34. Sadly, Fidrych was the lone bright spot that year, with those Tigers finishing next to last in the AL East in 1976. In addition, overuse of the young Fidrych's arm (he pitched a hefty 250 innings, and a league-leading but rookie-arm-destroying 24 complete games) ruined the promising pitcher's career.

From 1979 to 1995, the team was managed by the colorful George "Sparky" Anderson, one of baseball's winningest managers. When Sparky came on board, he made the bold move of predicting a pennant winner within five years (Sparky was voted into the Hall of Fame in 2000).

The first major news of the 1984 season actually came in late 1983, when long-time owner and broadcasting magnate John Fetzer, who had owned the club since 1957, sold the team to Domino's Pizza founder and CEO Tom Monaghan. The sale of the franchise caught everyone by surprise, as the negotiations culminating in the sale occurred in total secrecy away from the media. There were no rumors or even speculation that Fetzer had put the franchise up for sale.

After acquiring the team, Monaghan told reporters that buying the team fulfilled his childhood dream of owning the Detroit Tigers. However, the pizza magnate probably didn't think that he would win a World Series the first year he owned the team. However, the 1984 Tigers did just that, thereby going beyond Monaghan's wildest fantasies. The team led its division wire-to-wire, from Opening Day and every day thereafter, culminating in an ALCS sweep of the Kansas City Royals and a World Series victory over the San Diego Padres.

The 1984 team started out at a record 35-5 pace (including Jack Morris throwing a no-hitter early in the season against the Chicago White Sox), and cruised to a franchise-record 104 victories. That team featured the great double-play combination of shortstop Alan Trammell and second baseman Lou Whitaker; the duo would play together a record 19 seasons. The team also included Darrell Evans, Dave Bergman, Kirk Gibson, Chet Lemon, Larry Herndon, Morris, Dan Petry, Dave Rozema, Johnny Grubb, the late Aurelio Lopez ("Senor Smoke"), and relief ace Willie Hernandez, who won the 1984 American League Cy Young Award and Most Valuable Player just one year after pitching on the Philadelphia Phillies' National League championship club.

In 2006, the Detroit Tigers became the current American League Champions. Mike Ilitch, founder of Little Caesars Pizza and owner of the NHL's Detroit Red Wings, has owned the team since 1992. The Tigers were the runners-up of Major League Baseball in 2006, having lost in the World Series to the St. Louis Cardinals.

To the end, Marjorie remained loyal to the Detroit Tigers, even though she seldom spoke about them, for fear someone might ask about 'Hammerin Hank.' He of course was the one topic she preferred not to discuss during those final 62 years of her life. There was likely one exception to this—a situation that occurred only when she and her mother were together in private. Laura Eager Nash passed away in 1990, and I believe both of them were confident their 'Well-Kept Secret' would remain their secret evermore.

Down through the years Marjorie attempted to forget the good times she used to have with Hank and at times likely nearly succeeded. She certainly was and remained a wonderful wife and mother to the end. The three of us, Darrell, Debbie, and I, have many great memories of her and are proud to remember Marjorie Nash Klein, their mother and my wife, with lots of love.

In conclusion, we in the Klein family are very proud, of both Marjorie and Hank Greenberg. We are proud of the fact that she was amply persistent to eventually make an acquaintance with Henry. We are also proud of Hank now that we have studied his life, and certainly would have welcomed him into our lives as a friend had we been given the opportunity.

We are indeed fortunate to have so many good memories. Were Marjorie here today, she would most certainly be trying to help us tell her story correctly. And she would be working along with us to get her story to the publisher as soon as possible. ***God is Good.*** We do thank ***Him*** for letting Marjorie be such an important part of our lives down through the years.

More Tiger Memories

There are other Detroit Tiger Team players from the 'Glory Years' not included in the preceding pages. These men were also an important part of those great teams of the Hank Greenberg era:

CATCHERS:
Ray Hayworth
Paul Richards
Bob Swift
Birdie Tebbetts

PITCHERS:
Al Benton
George Carter
Alvin Crowder
Harry Eisenstat
Carl Fischer
Rufe Gentry
George Gill
Johnny Garsica
Luke Hamlin
Fred Hutchinson
Chief Hogsett
Roxie Lawson
Archie McKain
Fred 'Firpo' Marbarry
Les Mueller
Hal Newhauser
Stubby Overmire
Boots Poffenberger
Vic Sorrell
Joe Sullivan
Bud Thomas
Dizzy Trout
Vergil Trucks
Jake Wade
Hal White

FIRST BASE:
Jack Burns

SECOND BASE:
Jimmy Bloodworth
Eddie Mayo

THIRD BASE:
Dick Bartell
Frank Croucher
Billy Hitchcock
Joe Hoover
Eddie Lake
Skeeter Webb

OUTFIELD:
Earl Averill
Bruce Campbell
Doc Cramer
Roy Cullenbine
Hoot Evers
Pete Fox
Ned Harris
Barney McCosky
Eddie Mierkowitz
Chet Morgan
Jimmy Outlaw
Rip Radcliff
Al Simmons
Dick Wakefield
Dixie Walker
Gee Walker
Gerry Walker
Jo-Jo White

Ty Cobb was the first baseball player to be voted into the Hall of Fame. Known as the "Georgia Peach" Cobb played 22 seasons from 1905 to 1926, doubling as manager for the last six years. He was retired from the game by the time Marjorie's story began but was considered one of baseball's greats. Here are a few quotations from and about Ty Cobb supplied by the Baseball Almanac:

- "A ball bat is a wondrous weapon."
- "I never could stand losing. Second place didn't interest me. I had a fire in my belly."
- "The base paths belonged to me, the runner. The rules gave me the right. I always went into a bag full speed, feet first. I had sharp spikes on my shoes. If the baseman stood where he had no business to stand and got hurt, that was his fault."
- "When I began playing the game, baseball was about as gentlemanly as a kick in the crotch."
- "When I came to Detroit I was just a mild-mannered Sunday school boy."
- "Every great batter works on the theory that the pitcher is more afraid of him than he is of the pitcher."
- "I had to fight all my life to survive. They were all against me, but I beat the bastards and left them in the ditch."

Here are some quotations about Ty Cobb from his fellow baseball players:

- "Every time I hear of this guy again, I wonder how he was possible." ***—Joe DiMaggio***
- "(Ty) Cobb is a prick. But he sure can hit. God Almighty, that man can hit." ***—Babe Ruth***
- "He didn't outhit and he didn't outrun them, he out thought them." ***—Sam Crawford***
- "The greatness of Ty Cobb was something that had to be seen, and to see him was to remember him forever." ***—George Sisler***
- "I never saw anyone like Ty Cobb. No one even close to him. He was the greatest all time ballplayer. The guy was superhuman, amazing." ***—George 'Casey' Stengel***

EPILOGUE

The three Kleins, Darrell, Debbie, and the author, visited the National Baseball Hall of Fame in Cooperstown, N.Y in July of 2006. This is a marvelous institution for every baseball fan to enjoy. The main hall contains plaques of 266 of the best baseball players in the history of the game.

Ten Tigers from past years are among those we admired in the Hall of Fame. This exclusive group from Detroit and the year each was voted into the Hall are as follows:

1.	Tyrus Raymond Cobb	1936
2.	Mickey Cochrane	1947
3.	Charlie Gehringer	1949
4.	Harry Heilmann	1952
5.	Hank Greenberg	1956
6.	'Goose' Goslin	1968
7.	Al Kaline	1980
8.	George Kell	1983
9.	Hal Newhauser	1992
10.	Jim Bunning	1996

Also in the Hall of Fame, although not players, are broadcaster ***Ernie Harwell*** and Tiger Manager ***George 'Sparky' Anderson.***

Bibliography

Richard Bak. *Cobb Would Have Caught It. The Golden Age of Baseball in Detroit.* Wayne State University Press. 1993

Malcolme W. Bingay. *Detroit Is My Home Town.* 1946

Hal Butler. *Al Kaline and the Detroit Tigers*. Henry Regnery Company. 1973

Bob Feller and Burton Rocks. *Bob Feller's Little Black Book of Baseball Wisdom.* Contemporary Books. 2001

Hank Greenberg with Ira Berkow. *Hank Greenberg: The Story of My Life*. Triumph Books. 2001

Tom Keegan. *Ernie Harwell: My 60 Years in Baseball.* Triumph Books. 2005

John Sickels. *Bob Feller.* Beassey's, Inc. 2004

INDEX

Italics indicate autographed portraits